the
hymn texts
of
fred kaan

stainer and bell

hope publishing company

First published in 1985 by
Hope Publishing Company, Carol Stream, Illinois 60188, USA
and
Stainer & Bell Ltd, 82 High Road, London N2 9PW, England

Kaan, Fred
    The hymn texts of Fred Kaan
    1. Hymns, English
    I. Title
    264'.2   BV350

ISBN 0 85249 644 3 (World except USA and Canada)

Printed in Great Britain by Galliard (Printers) Ltd, Great Yarmouth

In the city full of people,
world of speed and hectic days,
in the ever-changing setting
of the latest trend and craze,
Christ is present, and among us
in the crowd we see him stand:
in the bustle of the city
Jesus Christ is Everyman

For Elly
Martin
Peter
Alison
and other
ecumenical
pilgrims

Contents

Introducing Fred Kaan

Fred Kaan was born on July 27th, 1929 in a terraced house in the Voorhelmstraat, a tree-less street in the North Holland city of Haarlem. He is the elder son of Herman Kaan and Brandina Kaan-Prinsen. His father started work as an apprentice-draughtsman on the Netherlands Railways, rising to the rank of safety inspector by the time he retired.

Fred's family was only nominally Christian and from the time he was baptised Frederik Herman in the great St. Bavo Cathedral in Haarlem until his late teens, he never set foot in church, although he did spasmodically attend a Sunday School. When he was 5, the family moved to Amersfoort where Fred began Primary School. Three years later, another move took the Kaans to Zeist, famous for its eighteenth century Moravian settlement. Here Fred completed his primary education and attended High School, with mathematics and sciences his chosen emphases, though later it was to Art College that he planned to go with the intention of being a painter.

Fred's Religious Education teachers in High School were three local ministers of the Reformed Church, each of whom went on to become a professor of theology at one of the Dutch State Universities. These men, among them Professor Doctor Hendrikus Berkhof, were to awaken in their pupil an interest in the church and in theology.

The years of early adolescence coincided with the Nazi occupation of Holland. His father was a member of the Dutch Resistance, and for two years the Kaans sheltered a Jewish woman in their home, and later gave refuge to an escaped political prisoner. His mother narrowly escaped death through starvation, thanks to special Red Cross teams being allowed into occupied Holland early in 1945 to deal with the most severe cases of undernourishment. But three grandparents died through lack of food during the 'hunger-winter' which lasted from the failure of the battle of Arnhem in September 1944 until the day of liberation on May 5th, 1945.

Fred met Elly Steller at school. They were to become engaged in 1949 and to marry in 1954. Elly was born on the remote Indonesian island of Sangir, daughter of missionaries, the Reverend K. G. F. Steller and Elisabeth Steller-Huvers. Her father died in a Japanese camp during the war and Elly was repatriated to Holland in 1946. Fred and Elly have three children: Martin, Peter and Alison, and one grand-daughter, Swedish-born Helena, daughter of Martin and Ingmarie.

It was in his late teens with the war over that Fred began to attend young people's worship services in Zeist. After about two years' regular attendance, he was invited to join the committee responsible for organising these services. At the same time, he started confirmation classes at the High School, led by Professor Doctor J. M. van der Linde, which led to Fred's reception into membership of the Netherlands Reformed Church in 1947.

At this time, leaving aside the mathematics and science of early High School and the plans for Art School, Fred was drawn to offer for the ministry and applied for admission to the theological faculty of the State University of Utrecht. To qualify for entrance to this faculty, he had to top up his High School diploma with a State supplementary examination in Latin and Greek. It was 1949 that he passed this hurdle and theological studies began in earnest.

Meantime, an early international link in Fred's life was being forged by a pen-friendship under the auspices of the post-war Boy Scouts' 'Linking-up Scheme' with a British lad living on the North-Eastern outskirts of London. This contact with a London family and an article on the subject of Congregationalism by Karl Barth in the journal *Die Schrift und die Kirche* during Fred's studies at Utrecht destined him to leave Holland. When the Boy Scout's father, a deacon in the local Congregational Church at South Woodford, spoke that throw-away 'Macedonian' line, 'Why don't you come over and help us?', Fred felt the conviction growing that here was a call that should be explored. So in 1952, having offered himself for the Congregational ministry, he left Holland and entered the Western College, Bristol, graduating at Bristol University in 1954.

After a post-graduate year which included sociology and pastoral studies, Fred was called to be minister of Windsor Road Congregational Church in Barry, South Wales and ordained on July 6th, 1955. Here he began to foster those world-wide relationships which have been prominent throughout his ministry, with the establishment of strong links with the international student community in the United Kingdom. In the years at Barry (1955 - 1963), the church visitors' book has entries from no fewer than 52 different countries. When in 1961 Fred attended the Assembly of the International Congregational Council in Rotterdam, it was the beginning of an international church life in which by the end of 1984, he had visited well over 60 countries, used 97 different airlines and boarded nearly 600 flights!

A main theme in Fred's ministry has always been his awareness of the here-and-nowness of Christ, coupled with the *unity* of life (life *before* death and life *after* death), spirituality and activism, worship and service, creed and politics, faith and witness. The wholeness (the one-ness) of God cannot truly be reflected either in a divided church or in a broken world, so the search for Christian unity, and the struggle for the unity of human society are inextricably related as part of one indivisible commitment. This view of life has alerted Fred to the need for Christians to exercise their discipleship in 'the modern city', and has led him to believe that Christians should be totally committed to be agents of change and sign-posts of the Kingdom. In personal terms, this has meant involvement in the United Kingdom Housing Action Group, Shelter; in Amnesty International; the Campaign for Nuclear Disarmament and to his being a committed pacifist.

It was to the modern city of Plymouth that Fred was called in 1963 as minister of the Pilgrim Church. A year later he was appointed co-secretary of the Plymouth Council of Churches and was active in setting up the Plymouth branch of Shelter.

Pilgrim Church gave birth to the name *Pilgrim Praise* for its home-made hymn supplement. Fred's hymnwriting was born of necessity, out of the frustration of not finding what he wanted in the established hymnbook for next Sunday's worship, and out of his eagerness to put into words those things which were close to his heart and conscience, using the language of the present time. No one who is familiar with the Kaan texts will be surprised that he uses extensively a dictionary of etymology so that the full depth of meaning is wrested from each English word used. This book reveals by its contents both Fred's chosen emphases and the gaps which he found unfilled. There were few baptismal hymns and few hymns which bridged the gap between the celebration of the sacrament of communion and its implementation. It is not surprising therefore that one of the first texts Fred wrote was a post-communion hymn:

Now let us from this table rise
renewed in body, mind and soul;
with Christ we die and live again,
his selfless love has made us whole.

With minds alert, upheld by grace,
to spread the Word in speech and deed,
we follow in the steps of Christ,
at one with man in hope and need.

To fill each human house with love,
it is the sacrament of care;
the work that Christ began to do
we humbly pledge ourselves to share.

Then grant us courage, father God,
to choose again the pilgrim way
and help us to accept with joy
the challenge of tomorrow's day.

While in Plymouth, Fred undertook in 1964 a chaplaincy on a United States-bound emigrant liner, repeating a similar earlier assignment in 1961. In 1966 he again attended the Assembly of the International Congregational Council, this time meeting at Swansea in South Wales. Then in 1967, he attended the first International Congress on Religion, Architecture and the Visual Arts in New York. During his two local pastorates, he frequently took groups of churchmembers on ecumenical study tours to the Continent.

In 1968, Fred received the call to the office of Minister-Secretary of the International Congregational Council in Geneva, a post held until 1970, when that Council and the World Presbyterian Alliance merged to become the World Alliance of Reformed Churches. He became an executive secretary of the new body, with three specific responsibilities. In the area of communication he was editor of the four-language *Reformed Press Service* and managing editor of the quarterly journal

Reformed World. A second responsibility was in administering a small project programme whilst his third assignment involved the monitoring of human rights violations, especially in the area of religious liberties.

His period in Geneva involved many other roles. He was a member of the staff working group of the World Council of Churches for *Cantate Domino*, the international and ecumenical hymnal; he attended as an observer the assemblies of the All Africa Conference of Churches in 1974 and the Christian Conference of Asia in 1978; he advised on worship for the 5th and 6th Assemblies of the World Council of Churches in Nairobi and Vancouver; for the 1979 Assembly of the Conference of European Churches, and as a member of the preparatory committee for the 1980 Melbourne Conference on World Mission and Evangelism; he was a member of the Ecumenical Workshop for Information in Europe and of the Europe Projects Screening Group, Inter-Church Aid, Refugee and World Service of the World Council of Churches and the Conference of European Churches. He also found time to be text consultant for *New Songs of Asian Cities*, published by the Christian Conference of Asia, and to lecture on hymn writing in such countries as Canada, the United States of America, Romania, Hungary and Vanuatu. He also was a member of the production team of the monthly radio programme *Intervox* broadcast from the studio of the Ecumenical Centre at Geneva.

Such a life inevitably involved an abundance of committees: it is little wonder that Fred wrote during one of them:

> With fervent dedication,
> in talks and consultation,
> we prostitute the word.
> Conferring round the table,
> (a long way from that stable),
> we sit and serve the servant-Lord.
>
> While people starve in cities,
> we travel to committees
> until the kingdom come.
> We share a high allegiance,
> divide the world in regions;
> departments are our second home.

Yet who can say how many ideas have been communicated across frontiers, how many misconceptions corrected, how much active love generated by this contemporary Christian globe trotter? How often has the broken been mended and one-ness re-established?

In 1978, Fred was called back to England by the General Assembly of his Church, the United Reformed Church (a union of Congregationalists and Presbyterians achieved in 1972) to serve for seven years as Moderator of the West Midlands Province, where a major role has been to oversee the local churches and their ministers. His commitment to the international scene remained. He has served as a member of the Global/Europe Project Screening Group of Christian Aid, as a member of the World Church and Mission Committee of the United Reformed Church and in 1983 he was appointed Deputy Chairman of the Council for World Mission. He is a member of the Hymn Society of America and of the International Fellowship for Hymnological Research as well as being a member of the Hymn Society of Great Britain and Ireland.

In 1978 Fred received an honorary Th.D. from the Reformed Theological Academy in Debrecen, Hungary, in recognition of his merits in the fields of hymn-writing and ecumenical relations. The official citation referred to his 'powerful interpretation of the social dimension of the Gospel, and the compelling call of his hymns on our sense of responsibility for the social problems of human-kind'.

In 1984 he was awarded a Ph.D. in Religious Studies (with distinction) by the Geneva Theological College for his dissertation entitled 'Emerging Language in Hymnody'.

Fred lists as his hobbies jazz, painting, graphic design, and, believe it or not, travel!

At the time of writing at the beginning of 1985, the tasks ahead when he ends his period of office as Moderator are unclear. Typically, Fred has refused to let his name go forward for re-nomination for a further period of office, if only to counter the dangers of 'hierarchical thinking' in his church, whereby people tend to regard the moderatorial office as having reached the top of a 'ladder'. Said Fred in a statement to his Synod in 1984: 'I do not believe that such a ladder exists. The only way to move in the ministry is sideways. I am firmly committed to servant-leadership. There may be different forms of ministry, but they are of equal importance and of a complementary nature. I am not a career person, and the only way in which I feel I can make my point is by not arguing the case, but by doing: by giving up this particular phase of ministry in order to be open and receptive to whatever may be the next call'.

What is certain about Fred's future is its mobility as he continues to practise his calling committed to discipleship in the modern world-city, where 'Jesus Christ is Everyman'.

Bernard Braley
January 1985

Introduction

Most of the texts that have been brought together in this anthology have already been published in my books *Pilgrim Praise, Break not the Circle* and *Songs and Hymns from Sweden*. They have been incorporated in an untraceably large number of hymnals in the English speaking world, translated into over a dozen other languages, published in the form of sheet music and choir anthems, made available on several LP records, while some of this material has been used in the composition of a number of major cantatas.

Although therefore this material has already been — and is constantly being — tested in the context of congregational worship the world over, Sunday by Sunday, in the critiques by hymnologists and reviews that have appeared in numerous theological, hymnological and liturgical journals, the selection and collection of my hymn-texts in this anthology constitutes the first systematic attempt at making all this material available in one volume, and for the first time providing background notes for each text.

In some ways this anthology is bound to be an 'apologia pro mea vita': Sing a *new* song to the Lord! (Psalm 96). This is my excuse and my motivation. Here I stand; I can do no other than respond to the Gospel as I perceive it, 20th century man that I am. I present this work as coming from the pen of a practising hymn-writer, rather than that of a hymnologist. St. James in his letter (1:22) exhorts us to be *doers* of the word, poièteis logou.

The inescapable conclusion I must draw from this is that I should 'get on with the doing' of texts. I see myself as a craftsman rather than as an academic researcher or critical reviewer (even though, of necessity, the craft must be firmly embedded in the search for and research into truly contemporary ways of worshipping God and singing the faith). I simply have to be caught up in the poetry of the word (Word) — the word uttered and done.

In one of my hymns I put it like this:

> God the narrator
> logically speaking,
> in the beginning
> shaped the good earth.
> Out of his true love
> speaking-and-do love
> blossomed and grew love:
> life came to birth. **(45)**

Dr. Norman Goodall, in the fifteenth Joseph Smith Memorial Lecture, given on October 12, 1968, said:

> The poet or prose craftsman, dealing with meaning and expression, describing life, interpreting experience and searching for the apt word or phrase, is holding rendez-vous with the Word; and when, as the result of the craftsman's discipline and the artist's dedication, a word takes wings and communicates, displaying a quality of everlastingness, there is then a consonance between the Word and the words. The writer, the speaker or the singer has proved to be an authentic servant of the Word. [1]

Although Dr. Goodall was lecturing on the subject of preaching, his reference to writer/speaker/singer strikes me as most appropriate when thinking through the call that is issued to all believers to be 'authentic servants of the Word'. I was all the more gratified, therefore, when Dr. Carlton R. Young, of the Candler School of Theology, Emory University, Atlanta, USA, did me the honour of introducing me as 'the model of the emerging poet-theologian-teacher-preacher'.[2]

When Dr. Goodall later in his lecture referred to the high calling and privilege of the preacher, he issued challenges which I have conscientiously accepted for myself as poet-theologian-teacher-preacher:

> . . . the servant of Christ who has ears for words never forgets that when the Word took flesh, it took more than speech, and testified to the truth with its life as well as its

words . . . In the present predicament of mankind the Christian preacher must be more than ever alert to the peril of merely verbalising the Gospel . . . Yet the safeguard against this danger does not lie finally in the humility of self-examination or even in the rigours of self-discipline. It lies in the release that becomes ours when the word we preach becomes the promise we trust.[3]

The preacher-poet, as a member of, and debtor to, the 'beloved community', lives under a life-long obligation to try and articulate afresh — both in the realm of spirituality and of activism — what the contemporary Christian experience is all about, to sing the faith (inviting others to sing along with him/her), to rejoice in Christian doctrine, and constantly to translate and implement what he/she hears and sees, tastes, touches and smells.

Indebtedness

Duke Ellington, in his autobiography, *Music is my Mistress*, makes a point of voicing his indebtedness to those who stimulated and assisted him in the nearly fifty performances of his sacred concerts:

I have done so not as a matter of career, but in response to a growing understanding of my own vocation, and with the encouragement of many people . . . I have been fortunate to have been accepted on this team of dedicated men and women who work ceaselessly in the ecumenical movement to bring peace to the world we live in now, and to secure our future down at the end where all ends end.[4]

No one could have been more surprised than I at the overwhelming response my texts have received around the worshipping world. No one more than myself could so 'accidentally' have become a hymn-writer; all that has happened to me in this field has been a modest implementation of that 'growing understanding of my own vocation' as a minister of the Word of God, and with the encouragement of countless people in ever-widening ecumenical circles: my home and family, the local congregation and the wider councils of my church, and the world church in its internationalness and stimulating diversity.

Among these, I must single out a local congregation. My involvement in hymn-writing owes much of its origin and stimulus to that remarkable group of alert Christians at the Pilgrim Church in Plymouth, England, whose minister I was from 1963 to 1968. Without them, this book would never have come about. A local gathered community in an urbanised setting, articulate and selfless in their life and work, they stimulated me in helping to find – together with them – new ways of worship and service and contemporary idioms in which to write hymns. The general mood at the Pilgrim Church was one of remarkable agility of spirit, and eagerness to try out what had not been tried before. Two phrases from the Pilgrim vocabulary have stayed with me ever since. One was: 'In this church everything is possible'. The other: 'The only tradition we have is that we have no tradition'!

Once again, I make Norman Goodall's words mine, when in a paper read to the London Society for the Study of Religion, at the Athenaeum on June 3, 1980, he said:

> I know that revelation is not static, and to try to bind it when in fact we are only binding ourselves in some old imprisonment, is fatal to the progress of any pilgrim in search of God. So I try to maintain the hearing ear and this perceptive vision is not to conclude that what I do not happen to like or understand must have been devised without the descent of the dove.
>
> Further, there are developments in thought and expression, philosophical, theological, epistemological, linguistic, amidst which I find myself 'moving in worlds not realised' . . .[5]

As I look back over nearly thirty years in the ministry, and in the life of the church at the local, regional, national and international levels, then the thing that strikes me is the impression of an increased mobility coupled with a profound earthiness and a direct and economic human-ness, marking the thought-processes and experiences of the household of God almost everywhere.

I suspect that gone forever are the days of dogmatics by the dozen or the black leather-bound tome: by which I do not mean that the Church will cease to read or be enriched and nourished by the Karl Barths of our immediate or distant past, but that it is highly unlikely that the future vehicles of our faith will require anything other than the most modest — or even improvised — inspection pits.

The missionary Church of today is being blessed, increasingly and effectively, by the discovery of its own equivalent brand of intermediate or appropriate technology.

Characteristics of intermediate technology include that it is basic, that it makes optimum use of materials and resources that are already available locally, and that it emphasises that it is people who matter, rather than the process or the profit.

Ours is a time of mimeographed theology, of consultation findings, a section report here and there, an assembly message, an encounter, a television interview, a song, a litany, a demonstration. Ours is a time of colourful paper-back theology, of the Koyama meditation, of the Hans Küng newspaper article, the Corita cardboard box wall.

A former Archbishop of Canterbury, Dr. Donald Coggan, said at a meeting of the World Association for Christian Communication, in London, June 6, 1978, that yesterday's theology had become inadequate for today. He clearly did not mean to advocate that all that is of yesterday should be thrown out of the church window, but that we should respond in contemporary ways to the Gospel of the Risen Christ. By the same token and in similar ways I believe yesterday's hymnody to be inadequate for today. Inasmuch as worship, song and celebration are part of our response to the Gospel as it comes to us *today*, they will need to be fresh and different, honestly typical of our time, inspired by new theologies, new insights into the scriptures and also new understandings of, and involvement in, the world around us from which we cannot and must not distantiate ourselves.

It is, I suppose, typical of a writer like Johann Ernst Bode (1816 - 74) that he should have sung with some fear and resentment that 'the world is ever near . . .' I should like to think that some day someone will say that it was typical of Fred Kaan to sing:

> We thank you that our faith has found expression
> in walls that shelter those who worship here;
> help us to be a house of intercession
> and make us *glad* the world is ever near. (**121**)

xvii

or, as I have put it in my *Hymn in the First Person Singular*:

> Meanwhile I live and move and I am glad,
> enjoy this life and all its interweaving;
> each given day, as I take up the thread,
> let love suggest my mode, my mood of living. **(110)**

Where are we, flesh-and-blood people, to be the Church if not in the world, in the modern city (in England today only 2½ to 3 per cent of the population are engaged in farming), in the rubbing of shoulders with others who, like ourselves, have been created in the image of God?

New Hymn for a New Day

Among the many small and slender publications that have come out during the past twenty years, related to the Church's hymnody, there is one which I judge to be of considerable importance, but which appears to have been overlooked by all but the small circle of people who were subscribers of the World Council of Churches' quarterly journal *Risk*. One of the reasons why that particular issue is not better known than it should be, is no doubt due to the fact that the number of subscribers was lamentably low in any case, and that the budget made it impossible to go into a second printing even when it was discovered that the book was in great demand. And so *New Hymns for a New Day (Risk*, Vol.II, No.3, 1966) has become something of a collectors' item. Leading American songwriters Richard Avery and Donald Marsh trace the origins of their musical ministry to their confrontation with this book, which — they say — changed their lives and set them off on their present successful career.

The book is important not just because of the mere 44 new hymns and songs it contains (some of which are not particularly good), but because of six pages' worth of introduction by that remarkable Dutch *enfant terrible* of the world church, Albert van den Heuvel.

This is van den Heuvel at his best, and I shall summarise what he says, and partly quote him in full. His initial thesis is that it is the hymns which, repeated over and over again, form the container of much of our faith, and he reminds us how Father Gelineau once said that the most important activity of the Christian community, next to the eucharist, is congregational singing.

But then the problem arises, as it did with van den Heuvel, that we can talk about new theological insights until we think the cows come home, but as long as these insights are not translated into liturgical hymns and liturgical action (in the sense that leitourgia is public service!), they will never reach the people.

Says van den Heuvel:

It seems nonsense to me that we learn together a new corporate existence in community, but sing Sunday after Sunday: 'When *I* tread the verge of Jordan, bid *my* anxious fears subside', and so continue to emphasise the individualism of the 18th and 19th centuries. It is senseless to speak of the secular city and at the same time to keep singing: 'O come, Thou Key of David, come and open wide our heavenly home: make safe the way that leads on high and close the path to misery'.

It is dangerous to work for an urban faith and to sing on Sunday about nothing but nature. Where are the hymns that speak about the humanisation of the structures of our society? Where are the hymns that help us to express our new insights into the Kingship of God? Where are the hymns that show our fascination with the human-ness of Christ? Where are the hymns that express hope, not in heaven but on earth? . . .

We have hardly begun to purify our hymns from dualism, excessive metaphysics, orgies of ontology, egocentric pietism and Constantinian ecclesiology.

I don't want to ridicule what is dear to many people, but it is either comic or tragic to hear a congregation which speaks of its service and witness in the modern world sing about an ingrown concentration on their own salvation. It seems to me that our unrenewed hymnbook is a greater obstacle to the renewal of our churches than all our outdated theological utterances.[6]

We have come a long way since then. The past twenty years have seen a veritable explosion of hymn-writing, 'a new English renaissance in hymnody' (Erik Routley) in the very areas which van den Heuvel singles out as standing in need of drastic renewal.

It is in these areas that new language has emerged and is emerging. New language symbolising, reflecting and expressing, but also — the other way round — inspiring and influencing the vocabulary of all the honest-to-God theologies that have been given to the Church in the past few decades:

1. theologies that have brought humanity, society, the earth and the world into the context of the worshipping and agonising congregation, and onto the agenda of the responsive and responsible church-meeting; and

2. theologies that have led us to a deeper awareness than maybe ever before of the humanity and here-and-now-ness of Christ.

Obviously, it would be possible to sub-divide these two headings and identify other, more detailed, principles of demarcation, and speak of the emerging language of hymnody as reflecting very specific areas — such as those that are delineated by the emphases on the social gospel, by theologies of liberation, feminist theology, the experience of the church in urban industrial mission activities and community development projects, Christians' involvement in the peace movements, the appearance of new and exciting translations of the Bible, the phenomenal growth of international-ecumenical meetings, exchange and study, etc. For the purpose of this introduction, however, I intend to look simply at the two broad areas I have indicated above. At the same time I feel compelled, on the basis of personal experience in the field of producing new liturgical and hymnic material, to admit that new language is emerging for *negative* as well as for *positive* reasons. Negative — because of the way in which so often our hard-cover previous-generation hymnbooks have failed to enable us to sing what we believed we were led, and wanted, to sing in response to the love and goodness of God. Positive — precisely because we have been given new insights into that love and goodness for which humanity is crying out, and which we see embodied supremely in Jesus, the Man for others, and Lord of all.

As far as my own work is concerned, the negative motivation prompting me to reach out for, and uncover or cause to emerge, new hymnodic language, has come under all the headings van den Heuvel has listed, but, more specifically, it has often found its origin in my frustration and practical anger at the remote symbolism, the antiquated terminology and the socially unacceptable nature of much that was on offer. My day-to-day involvement in the life of the congregation and the modern city simply claimed me for that pro-test movement in favour of stressing within and together with the beloved community the *immanence of God* and the *real presence of Christ* in accessible, honestly contemporary English.

And so (though on the surface it sounds paradoxical) the first hymns I ever needed to write were inevitably communion and post-communion texts; after all it is around the Table that we recognise the Lord (etymologically: loaf-ward, the one who has it in his power to distribute bread to those who work for him!), who sends us out into a world broken by unshared bread. It is at this Table that we are at the very heart of the liturgy, the work of the *laos*, the whole people of God, who must be enabled to speak and sing in their own language of the great things God has done, rather than having theologically and historically remote jargon forced upon them.

Dr. Olle Engström, principal of the Lidingö Theological Seminary of the Swedish Mission Covenant Church, in his introduction to my *Songs and Hymns from Sweden*, usefully summarises the reasons for and characteristics of the new emerging language of hymnody:

> A common factor from country to country is the renewal in patterns of worship caused by the immense changes in the society in which the churches have to carry out their task . . . characteristic of the new texts is that they are not abstract systematic theology in rhyme, as was so often the case in the past. They proclaim the presence of God in the living Christ and the Spirit in the everyday life of men and women – even in the cities. There are more pavements, there is more smell of hectic rush hours than ever before in Christian hymnbooks, where the only city that was mentioned was the heavenly Jerusalem.
>
> The troubled hearts of men and women in this era of frustration – and God's concern not only for uncertain and

desolate individuals but for the whole of creation, . . .
these are among the main themes that occur.[7]

The World Writes the Agenda

Coming now to the two major areas I identified earlier, where new
hymnodic language is emerging as a result of the world being brought
into the consciousness of the worshipping and agonising church, and of
the creation of a deeper awareness of the very present humanity of
Christ, I should like to try and illustrate the former with a few texts or
text fragments from *Pilgrim Praise* and *Break Not the Circle*:

> Each year we sing with bated Christmas voice
> as if events in Bethlehem were 'nice',
> when every house and pub had shut its door
> and Mary in a shed her baby bore.
>
> Forgive us, Lord, that things are still the same,
> that Christ is homeless under other names:
> still holy fam'lies to our cities come
> where life is sick and sore in crowded slum.
>
> Lord, make it clear that joy will be denied
> unless the door into our life stands wide;
> that even with our tables richly spread
> our house of life is short of living bread. *
>
> Give us, O Father, restlessness of soul,
> till right is done and life is healed and whole;
> keep us impatient till the time has come
> when all your children are on earth at home. **(23)**

(* Beth-lehem = house of bread)

This hymn grew up when I became involved in the establishment of a
local 'Shelter' group in Plymouth, the housing action group.
    The next illustration is that of a harvest hymn, which was born
out of anger and frustration that accompany the annual experience of

going into the tunnel of harvest festivals. It begins in a traditional enough way, almost tongue in cheek:

> Now join we, to praise the creator,
> our voices in worship and song;
> we stand to recall with thanksgiving
> that to him all seasons belong.

But then, soon, the text comes down to the facts of life stripped of all the romanticism that so often marks harvest thanksgiving services:

> But also of need and starvation
> we sing with concern and despair,
> of skills that are used for destruction,
> of land that is burnt and laid bare.

> We cry for the plight of the hungry
> while harvests are left on the field,
> for orchards, neglected and wasting,
> for produce from markets withheld.

The remaining verses then try to point to the real application of the thanksgiving mood:

> The song grows in depth and in wideness:
> the earth and its people are one.
> There can be no thanks without giving,
> no words without deeds that are done.

> Then teach us, O Lord of the harvest,
> to be humble in all that we claim;
> to share what we have with the nations,
> to care for the world in your name. (78)

Biblical language in itself is not enough and its relevance in a general way needs to be supplemented with the type of language and insights that will enable the singing congregation to put side by side the eternal message of the scriptures and the haunting images we receive on television.

I am deeply grateful that so many of my texts that come into this category have been so widely adopted by the Christian church throughout the world, with an eagerness that both thrills and humbles me — like the *Hymn on Human Rights*, 'For the healing of the nations, Lord, we pray with one accord', with its strong prayer and determination that all that kills abundant living should be banned from this earth; or *Sing we of the modern city*, and *Magnificat Now!*, which so upset the Rt. Hon. Enoch Powell, M.P., and some of the West German Lutheran churchleaders.[8]

I believe with all my heart that this is the kind of language that needs to emerge today, as it speaks to the soul of the household of God, and with unmistakable directness proclaims a Christ who beyond statistics has shown that human life *is* crowned with glory, and who by his timeless presence proves that people *do* matter and count.

Alongside and accompanying all the specificity of modern terminology and vocabulary, it is essential to go back beyond and through the barriers of nineteen centuries of bible translations and church traditions that cloud our ability really to understand what the scriptures are saying to women and men today, in that remarkable directness and economy of that biblical language which employs only *one* word for speech and action!

Emerging language in hymnody will be most effective when the writer-craftsman has some modest facility for going back to rudimentary Hebrew and Greek with the help of a good dictionary; and when she or he reaches *as a matter of course* for the dictionary of English etymology — an exercise I warmly recommend to all whose responsibility it is regularly to preach the Word in our churches.

Christ in the Midst

Another dominant feature in my work is the emphasis I put on the humanity and here-and-now-ness of Christ, Word in human form. I have been more consistently criticised on this point than about any other facet of my work. The most subtle way in which the critique has come, was in the form of a question: 'Why don't you write hymns like *Immortal, invisible, God only wise*?' To which the only possible answer was that that had already been written!

Like Fred Pratt Green, I do not wish to 'computerise the

transcendent out of our religion', but the point is that we already have so many exciting texts emphasising the majesty and transcendence of God and the divinity of Christ, that I see it as part of my calling to try and articulate that the contemporary Christian experience *also* includes at its very heart the longing to respond to the person of Christ, that Man for others, the Lord of all.

Dr. T. F. Torrance, in his essay on *The Church in the New Era of Scientific and Cosmological Change* devotes substantial attention to the work of Joseph Andreas Jungmann, 'perhaps the greatest liturgiologist of the twentieth century':

> Jungmann has revealed, with meticulous examination, and documentation, a process of increasing liturgical monophysitism (as I have called it) in the development of the Church's liturgies in East and West, that is, a movement of greater and greater stress on the deity and majesty of Christ in worship together with diminishing room for the priesthood of the man Jesus . . . Christ became so pushed into the sheer majesty of God that worshippers lost sight of his humanity in its vicarious and priestly role in human worship of the Father.[9]

Torrance then continues to speak of more recent instances of a recovered stress upon the vicarious humanity or human priesthood of Jesus as evidenced in Roman Catholic piety as well as in Evangelical piety:

> as it is expounded, for example, by Karl Barth who has singled out this aspect of the teaching of John Calvin for special development in his christology . . . Christ is discerned to be God come as man, ranging himself on the side of man toward the Father, and not merely from the side of the Father toward man, even in the most intimate and deeply human activities of faith, worship and prayer directed toward God.[10]

More recently I have been stimulated by Edward Schillebeeckx, the Dominican scholar, who in an interview spoke of the position he had adopted in his book *Jesus - an experiment in Christology*:

> I tried to help people to grasp how Jesus was experienced
> by his contemporaries. Jesus shows us what God will be for
> us and also what man must be for God. I do not deny that
> Jesus is God, but I want to assert that he is also man,
> something that has been overlooked. It is precisely as a man
> that he is important for us . . . When you try to make the
> Chalcedonian formulas come alive for people today, you
> discover a Christ who puts down the mighty and gives the
> poor first place. Yes, that can be revolutionary . . .

There is no need to stress how delighted I was when Tom Harpur,
religious editor of the *Toronto Star*, headed an article about my work
with the words: Hymn-writing revolutionary.[11]

Sometimes it is gratifying to see other people come to one's
defence. Fred Pratt Green, at the 1980 Annual Conference of the
Hymn Society of Great Britain and Ireland, said about my texts:
'their strength is that they *are* hymns, that they are Christian hymns
in their unfailing acknowledgment of God as the source of all good,
and of Christ as not only the Man for others, but as Lord. He is
sufficiently true to our Christian tradition to enable us to sing his
hymns without a sense of betrayal of our faith, or a weakening of it'[12]
In moments of self-doubt, this kind of comment gives me new courage
and encouragement.

Maybe at the heart of my experience of the Risen Christ in my
contemporary world is the message of what has been called the 'most
Protestant of all Christian festivals', namely the neglected feast of the
Ascension. I have wrestled with it and come up with the following:

> Although our Lord has left us,
> he leaves us not alone.
> 'ascended into heaven',
> he makes the earth his home.
> He is alive and present
> and makes us all akin;
> in every human being
> he walks the world again.

By going to the Father,
he makes his choice for man.
In him who shaped the cosmos
humanity is one.
The candle is extinguished
and yet the light remains:
he who enlightens people
is in our midst and reigns. (3)

The Lordship of Christ, so poorly celebrated by so many Christians on Ascension Day, is given its clearest profile in the way he humbled himself in life and death, identifying himself with the life and death of women, children and men, not just historically, but timelessly. Here is enduring down-to-earth-ness, here-and-now-ness; kairos overriding chronos, appointed time overruling linear time.

Our Lord becomes incarnate
in every human birth.
Created in his image,
we *must* make peace on earth.
God will fulfil his purpose
and this shall be the sign:
we shall find Christ among us
as women, child or man. (111)

This is part of an Advent hymn, one of several illustrations of my understanding of my calling to try and help worshipping congregations to see the presence of God in Christ, not just historically, but contemporarily, much in the same way that people may come to 'see' the point of a story or a joke, and be surprised by joy.

The new language which I see emerging, and want to help emerge in the church's hymnody and worship is a celebratory language that bears within itself the vocabulary of commitment to the people of today and to their world, to the earth and its precarious life, and to God and his Christ. It is the language of the faith that believes not merely in life *after* death, but in life *before* death; the language of 'Christ-conscious praise and prayer, in a vernacular "understanded by the people", enabling a new generation to sing with integrity'. (Norman Goodall).

If I were told that only one of my texts could survive, I would fervently hope that it might be the one that owes its inspiration to St. John and Duke Ellington. The latter, in his autobiography, *Music is my Mistress*, begins with a bar of music and those basic words: 'In the beginning: God!'.[13] It is later in his book, where he writes about civilisation, seeing God, and sacred concerts, that he describes unconditional love as not only meaning 'I am with you, but I am also for you, all the way, right or wrong'.[14]

The hymn in question is *A Hymn of First, Last and In-Between*. It deals with the unending and unbegun nature of God, and at the same time with what I would underline as one of the main themes I have constantly highlighted in my writings, namely that of the immediacy of human existence, wholly interwoven with the real presence of Christ in contemporary life. The fact that *'now* is the time of our life' **(97)** receives so much emphasis in my work is integrally related to that greatest given-ness of all time: 'I am Alpha and Omega, the beginning and the end'. (Revelation 21:6)

The typical risk and excitement of ad-hoc discipleship are firmly embedded in the knowledge that God is not only with us, but that He is here-and-now with us; so that is how I have tried to 'place' humanity:

> The great between is now
> and time is ours to tell.
> God comes and tells us how
> to stand and walk and spell.
> So life becomes a feast,
> a round to set us free,
> for God is first and last
> and in-between are we! **(56)**

Fred Kaan
Kenilworth
November 1984

FOOTNOTES

1 *I believe in words*, Norman Goodall, The Berean Press, Birmingham, 1968, p.6
2 *The Hymn*, Hymn Society of America quarterly, October 1977, p.180
3 *I believe in words*, Norman Goodall, The Berean Press, Birmingham, 1968, p.12
4 *Music is my Mistress*, Duke Ellington, W. H. Allen, London, and Doubleday & Co. Inc. New York for USA, 1977, p.267
5 From a photocopy of Dr. Norman Goodall's address to the June 1980 meeting of the London Society for the Study of Religion: Words, Music, God, some reflections on the relation between aesthetic experience and knowledge of God. p.18
6 *New Hymns for a New Day, Risk* Vol. II, No. 3, 1966, World Council of Churches, p.6
7 *Songs and Hymns from Sweden*, Stainer & Bell, London, 1976
8 Hymn No. 93 in *Hymn Texts of Fred Kaan*
9 *Theology in Reconciliation*, Essays by Thomas F. Torrance, Geoffrey Chapman, a division of Cassell Ltd, 1975, p.287
10 ibid p.228
11 *The Toronto Star*, January 26th, 1974
12 The original text of an address to the Hymn Society at the Conference of 1979 and summarised in an article on 'The Social Gospel in Modern Hymnody' in *The Bulletin*, The Hymn Society of Great Britain and Ireland, Vol. IX, No.5, 1980, p.137
13 *Music is my Mistress*, Duke Ellington, W. H. Allen, London, and Doubleday & Co. Inc. New York for USA, 1977, p.2
14 ibid p.266

A note on inclusive language

All the texts in this anthology have been carefully scrutinised and where this has been possible, sexist language has been replaced by inclusive wording. Readers familiar with my original texts, especially those contained in *Pilgrim Praise*, will notice that considerable amendments have been made. Those familiar with my later writings will have noticed that they show a clear progression towards inclusiveness. As I look back over the years I am aware that I needed to go through processes of conscientisation and growth in sensitivity.

Ron Klusmeier, in his liner notes on the record sleeve of *Look Beyond* (The Gentle Clowns, No. 3192), observes:

> One of the exciting aspects of the faith is the way in which our perceptions and understandings change and grow. Our generation has witnessed an increased sensitivity to the issue of language and the importance of being as inclusive as possible as we choose the words we write and speak. For those of us involved in creating new worship resources, this has brought with it a heightened awareness of the new words we write, and wherever possible, revisions of earlier works.
>
> The obvious difficulties encountered in revisions include maintaining the intent and integrity of the original text without sacrificing rhyme scheme, rhythm, flow and metre.

Most of my writing has proved capable of amendment, but some of it has not, in which case I would plead that singers will go in for what I would call 'back-of-the-head-asterisk-singing'.

As a Free Churchman, I am not in the regular habit of repeating creeds in worship, but whenever I am in the company of those whose custom it is to recite the historic creeds, I happily join them, albeit with a number a 'mental reservations and footnotes'. It could be so with some of the hymns we sing: where words cannot be changed for irrefutable reasons, we could surely sing them and think inclusively as we do so!

F.K.

ROUND-TABLE CHURCH.

The church is like a table,
a table that is round.
It has no sides or corners,
no first or last, no honours;
here people are in one-ness
and love together bound.

The church is like a table
set in an open house;
no protocol for seating,
a symbol of inviting,
of sharing, drinking, eating;
an end to "them" and "us".

The church is like a table,
a table for a feast
to celebrate the healing
of all excluded-feeling,
(while Christ is serving, kneeling,
a towel round his waist).

The church is like a table,
where every head is crowned.
As guests of God created,
all are to each related;
the whole world is awaited
to make the circle round.

Fred Kaan.
Dec. 14. 1984

Written on the 7.40 Coventry to Euston.
© 1985. Hope Publishing Company for the USA
and Canada, and Stainer and Bell Ltd
for other territories.

449

現代都市歌
SING WE OF THE MODERN CITY

僅託順服

黃永熙譯，1974
Frederik Herman Kaan, b. 1929
E♭調

Henry Smart, 1813-1879

$\frac{4}{4}$ 3 6 5 | 3 | 1·2 1 7 | 6·5 | 1 3 | 5 4 3 2 – | 3 6 5 3 | 1·2 1 7 |

6 5 1 | 4 | 3 2 1 – | 2 5 | 5 ♯4 | 3 3 3 2 | 2 7 6 3 | 5 ♮4 5 – |

7 5 i | 5 | 4· 5 | 4 3 | 6 5 | 4 3 | 2 2 1 – | 1 1 – 1 – ‖

1. 我們唱歌現代都市，壓力歡笑相對照，我們唱歌在茫羣眾，
   市區彷如野荒郊；千憧萬戶櫛比相連，生活多姿變無窮，
   人生巨輪旋轉不停，生老病死每日同。

2. 都市繁榮萬頭攢擁，高速緊張人忙，五花八門變幻多端，
   縱住新潮如瘋狂；惟獨基督與眾同在，安然站在人叢中，
   鬧市生活熙熙攘攘，基督與眾息息通。

3. 上帝不居遙遠天空，在地分擔人羞恥，祂把無倚數字圖表，
   使有人性有名字；基督表明統計數外，人人生命皆貴重；
   永恆主宰同在，體貼關懷為大眾。（阿們）。

From *Hymns of Universal Praise* (1978). Chinese translation by W. Heyward Wong.

The Reverend Dr. Fred Kaan

Photograph: Rosa Fortunato

1 A minimal hymn

7.7.7.7.5 5.

All that Christians have in life
is a story and a song;
bread and wine, a little faith
and a longing to belong.
  That is all they have,
  that is all they have.

All that Christians are in life:
they are people of 'the way',
led by hunches, lured by hope,
now excited, then afraid.
  That is what they are,
  that is what they are.

All that Christians have and are
is a picture of their Lord,
is a signal and a glimpse,
is a gesture and a word.
  That is where they are,
  that is where they are.

It was a casual remark by Albert van den Heuvel, the (then) general secretary of the Netherlands Reformed Church, that triggered off this text. We were both present at the 1976 General Assembly of the Indonesian Council of Churches in Salatiga, Java, as ecumenical observers. During a particularly complex and highly technical debate on organisational re-structuring, Dr. van den Heuvel whispered to me: ' . . . and then to think that all we have as Christians is a piece of bread, a sip of wine and a song; those are the basics'. Dr. Philip Potter general secretary of the World Council of Churches, later suggested the hymn's title. Although frequently sung at worship events in the ecumenical centre, Geneva, to a calypso-style tune by the Jamaican composer, Doreen Potter, the hymn was not introduced to a wider circle until 1980, when it appeared in *Choirbook for Saints and Singers* with a melody CREDO by the book's editor, Carlton R. Young.

2 Almond blossom—sign of life

Almond trees, renewed in bloom,
do they not proclaim
life returning year by year,
love that will remain?

Almond blossom, sign of life
in the face of pain,
raises hope in people's hearts:
spring has come again.

War destroys a thousand-fold,
hatred scars the earth,
but the day when almonds bloom
is a time of birth.

Friends, give thanks for almond blooms
swaying in the wind:
token that the gift of life
triumphs in the end.

This is a translation of the original German text by Schalom Ben-Chorin. West-German composer Fritz Baltruweit, who was one of the music animators at the 1983 Vancouver Assembly of the World Council of Churches, asked me, while there, if I could translate the text: 'Freunde, dass der Mandelzweig wieder blüht und treibt'. As it was urgent, I managed to do the translation within half an hour. It was sung to a tune MANDELZWEIG composed by Baltruweit himself, first published by the Lutherisches Verlagshaus, Hanover, and incorporated in the 1983 *Kirchentag* hymnbook. Another possible tune is BEMERTON.

3 A hymn for Ascension—quote, unquote

7.6.7.6.D.

Although our Lord has left us,
he leaves us not alone.
'Ascended into heaven',
he makes the earth his home.
He is alive and present
and makes us all akin;
in every human being
he walks the world again.

By going to the Father,
he makes his choice for man.
In him who shaped the cosmos
humanity is one.
The candle is extinguished
and yet the light remains;
he who enlightens people,
is in our midst and reigns.

In many Catholic/Orthodox Christian churches the paschal candle is extinguished on Ascension Day, after the gospel reading in the mass. The reference 'The candle is extinguished' in the text is a deliberate introduction of this liturgical practice into what has sometimes been called 'that most protestant of all Christian festivals'. The use of quotation marks in the text is, of course, equally deliberate; they ought to be used more widely in matters of Christian doctrine! The hymn was written for the Pilgrim Church, Plymouth, which I served from 1963 - 68. It was an attempt to 'deal with' the story of the Ascension, and also as a kind of response to the introduction of the word 'ascendancy' by Bishop John Robinson of *Honest to God* fame. It can be found in *Pilgrim Praise* with the seventeenth century tune by Teschner ST. THEODULPH and with a modern tune INVISIBLE PRESENCE by H.W. Holmsen.

4 A hymn on spelling glory

8.7.8.7.
and chorus 7 7.

As the glory of creation
and the thrill of human love,
as the wonder at a cradle,
at the things that live and move,
higher still, uncaught in word,
is the glory of the Lord.

As the glory of a concert
and the skill of those who play,
as the joy of book and painting,
shapes in stone and bronze and clay,
Chorus

As the glory of the future
and the teaching of the past,
as the challenge of the present
and the here-and-now of Christ,
Chorus

In the life and work of Jesus,
in his dying on a cross,
in the great surprise of Easter
giving people gain for loss,
here we catch and taste the Word
spelling glory to the Lord.

This hymn arose out of reflections at the Centenary Consultation of the World Alliance of Reformed Churches in St. Andrews, Scotland in 1977. The theme was 'The Glory of God and the Future of Man'. Composer and Church of Scotland minister Douglas Galbraith, now professor of pastoral theology at St. Stephen's College, Brisbane, Australia, composed a tune for it during the Consultation, naming it INGRID after my (then) secretary, Mrs. Ingrid Trigo-Trindade. The hymn was first sung during the Consultation, and was later published in the quarterly journal of the World Alliance of Reformed Churches, *Reformed World*.

5 A communion hymn

5.6.6.4.

As we break the bread
and taste the life of wine,
we bring to mind our Lord
Man of all time.

Pass from hand to hand
the living love of Christ!
Machines and people raise
bread for this feast.

Grain is sown to die;
it rises from the dead,
becomes through human toil
our common bread.

Jesus binds in one
our daily life and work;
he is of all mankind
symbol and mark.

Having shared the bread
that died to rise again,
we rise to serve the world,
scattered as grain.

When Jesus said that he is the bread of life, I believe that he not only meant that our need of him is as basic as our need of bread, but that he was also hinting at broader truths, referring to the whole intense process of natural growth, human labour and market forces that play a role in bringing bread to our tables and altars. The eucharist may be a mystery, but bread never appears mysteriously at the communion. In that sense, Jesus does sum up all of life, from hard work to spiritual devotion and vice versa. Written for the Pilgrim Church originally, this text received its first wider airing in 1971 in *The Canadian Hymnbook* in which it appeared to a tune MASSON composed especially by Stanley L. Osborne, secretary of the Hymnbook committee. Erik Routley hailed this tune as one of the finest examples of a melody fitting the words like a glove. A tune ST. MACHAR was written by E. Sangster for *Songs for the Seventies*, a Church of Scotland publication; BROKEN BREAD composed by Patty Evans was published in *Hymnal Supplement*.

6 Komm Herr, segne uns

11.11.11.11.

Bless, and keep us, Lord, in your love united,
from your family never separated.
You make all things new as we follow after;
whether tears or laughter, we belong to you.

Blessing shrivels up when your children hoard it;
help us, Lord, to share, for we can afford it:
blessing only grows in the act of sharing,
in a life of caring, love that heals and glows.

Fill your world with peace, such as you intended.
Teach us prize the earth, love, replenish, tend it.
Lord, uplift, fulfil all who sow in sadness:
let them reap with gladness, by your kingdom thrilled.

You renew our life, changing tears to laughter;
we belong to you, so we follow after.
Bless and keep us, Lord, in your love united,
never separated from your living Word.

This is a straight translation of a German text written by that prolific
hymnwriter and composer Dieter Trautwein, Provost of Frankfurt,
Federal Republic of Germany. The original was first introduced at
the 1979 Kirchentag in Nuremberg to a melody FRANKFURTER
SEGENSLIED composed by Dr. Trautwein. I first introduced it to the
English-speaking world during a 'Kaan Hymn Festival' at the 1980
Convocation of the Hymn Society of America, at the Westminster
Choir College, Princeton, New Jersey.

7 Song, circling all the earth

6.6.6.6.6.6.5.

Bread, feeding people's hope,
joy, cheering human souls,
song, circling all the earth,
shelter, that keeps us safe,
ears, catching sounds of life,
song, circling all the earth,
circling all the earth.

Words, in the silence heard,
drink, quenching people's thirst,
song, circling all the earth,
rain, chasing drought away,
child, showing us the way,
song, circling all the earth,
circling all the earth.

Power, making bodies strong,
hands that help the weak along,
song, circling all the earth,
bread, that will multiply,
care, spent on humankind,
song, circling all the earth,
circling all the earth.

A translation of a German song by Wilhelm Willms to music SONG CIRCLE by Peter Janssens. The translation was made during and for the Fifth Assembly of the World Council of Churches in Nairobi, 1975, where it was frequently used, especially at the exhilarating late night and early morning celebrations led by Peter Janssens and his 'Song Orchestra', who made such a vital contribution to the Assembly's worship life. The English version later appeared to a new melody by American composer Ron Klusmeier on an LP entitled *Song circling all the earth* (Praise Records PRC 369) and was first introduced to a world-wide audience in a BBC overseas broadcast, in the series *Reflections* in October 1980.

8 A hymn on not breaking the circle

10.11.10.11.

Break not the circle of enabling love,
where people grow, forgiven and forgiving;
break not that circle, make it wider still,
till it includes, embraces all the living.

Come, wonder at this love that comes to life,
where words of freedom are with humour spoken
and people keep no score of wrong and guilt,
but will that human bonds remain unbroken.

Come, wonder at the Lord who came and comes
to teach the world the craft of hopeful craving
for peace and wholeness that will fill the earth:
he calls his people to creative living.

Join then the movement of the love that frees,
till people of whatever race or nation
will truly be themselves, stand on their feet,
see eye to eye with laughter and elation.

In reply to questions about how long it takes to complete a text, I have to give varying answers. Normally, it is a matter of long hours and meticulous revision processes. In the case of this hymn, however, it only took me twenty minutes to write, in circumstances that can be described as 'at least distracting'. I wrote this text by the side of a swimming pool at a Romanian resort, surrounded by my then young daughter Alison and lots of her newly acquired friends, all claiming my attention. The urge to write this text was very strong and, once written, it was never revised. It later gave the title to a collection of new hymns *Break not the Circle* for which all the tunes were composed by Doreen Potter. Her tune has been named both CIRCLE and LEYTONEN.

9 While you have time and life

7 7.7 7.
and chorus 6.6 4.4 7.

Christian people, serve the Lord
with your actions and your word.
Work! And ask that God will bless
all the talents you possess.
  Praise God with every breath
  while you have time and life
    have time and life
  because the dead
  cannot praise our living head.

While the earth keeps turning round,
let your hope and faith abound;
love with body, mind and soul,
this you owe to God and all.
  Chorus

Use your talents for the Lord,
put to practice all you've heard;
there are those who will believe
through the way in which you live.
  Chorus

Translated, paraphrased and abbreviated from an original Bemba text
(Zambia) of Ronald Ndawa, who also composed the tune BEMBA, for
a worship event at the ecumenical centre in Geneva, 1969.

10 A hymn on Christ 'giving himself away'

10.10.10.10.

Christ is alive! — He gives himself away
where bread is broken at the eucharist
and his disarming Spirit can transform
to hungry hand the most dogmatic fist.

Christ is alive! — He gives himself away
wherever human beings drop their guard
and to each other look, reach out, in trust;
where dignity and bread are justly shared.

Christ is alive! — He gives himself away
where people pray and work for peace on earth,
un-learning prejudice in speech and thought,
and re-affirming human life and worth.

Christ is alive! — He gives himself away
where people rise to follow him in faith
and make their life a liturgy of love
to celebrate his triumph over death.

I wrote this text immediately after I had attended the Easter worship service at South Aston United Reformed Church, Birmingham in 1983. Its main theme, about Christ giving himself away, was triggered off by a recurring line in the minister's, Peter Loveitt's, prayer of invocation. A possible tune is BOROUGH by Cyril Taylor; it may be found in *Hymns and Psalms* where it is set to George Briggs 'Come risen Lord, and deign to be our guest'.

11 A hymn for Advent (or any other time when anticipation runs high!)

7 7.7 7.7 7.

Christ is coming, Christ has come,
let the world prepare a room.
God says: Light! and makes our day;
fear and chaos lose their say.
In our darkness shines our Sun:
God has made a date with man.

Christ has come, will come again,
parable of God-and-Man,
Lord of all our unborn days,
world-renewing turn of phrase,
Word in season for all time,
godly reason, godly rhyme.

Let the world make time and room
for the Man who is to come.
He, the centre of our feast,
makes himself of all the least.
Stones and voices all proclaim:
There is bread in Bethlehem!

The text stresses the timelessness of Advent, and the here-and-nowness of Christ. First published in *Break Not the Circle* in 1975 to a Doreen Potter tune, ADVENTURE, it is also included in the *Hymnal Supplement* to John Ness Beck's PREPARATION.

12 Celebration everywhere, any time

7.6.7.6.
(Trochaic)

Christ is crucified today,
Christmas is tomorrow.
Lent will fall in summertime,
Easter is to follow.

Christ is here and everywhere,
one with all his people,
but we mark his whereabouts
with our Sunday steeples.

Christ is Lord — we fence him out
from routine and Monday;
tie him down to holiness,
feasting, fasting, Sunday.

Lord, forgive our formal ways
and our special seasons;
free us from the faith that stills,
stifles or imprisons.

Make us whole and bind in one
reason and emotion,
let our life-style manifest
day-to-day devotion.

Give us grace to seize and use
every situation,
any time for worship, love,
blessing, celebration!

This hymn was especially written for a staff worship service at the ecumenical centre in Geneva to mark the beginning of Lent. The service was devised and led by staffmembers of the World Alliance of Reformed Churches, who, though not wanting to disregard Lent as such, also chose to emphasize the danger of 'special seasons'. The hymn jumbles up the sequences of the Christian Year and stresses - as so many texts in this anthology do - the real presence of Christ in the life of every day, whether churchly or secular. Doreen Potter wrote the tune CELEBRATION for *Break Not the Circle*. It also appears to Jane Marshall's NEW SEASON in the *Hymnal Supplement*.

13 Cristo vive!

8.7.8.7.D.

Christ is risen, Christ is living,
dry your tears, be unafraid!
Death and darkness could not hold him,
nor the tomb in which he laid.
Do not look among the dead for
one who lives for evermore;
tell the world that Christ is risen,
make it known he goes before.

If the Lord had never risen,
we'd have nothing to believe.
But his promise can be trusted:
'You will live, because I live'.
As we share the death of Adam,
so in Christ we live again.
Death has lost its sting and terror.
Christ the Lord has come to reign.

Death has lost its old dominion,
let the world rejoice and shout!
Christ the firstborn of the living
gives us life and leads us out.
Let us thank our God who causes
hope to spring up from the ground.
Christ is risen, Christ is giving
life eternal, life profound.

The original text is Spanish, written by Argentinian Nicolas Martines. This is one of several translations specially prepared for the 1973 edition of *Cantate Domino*, the international ecumenical hymnal which, in its first three editions, had been published under the auspices of the World Student Christian Federation, but which was later 'taken over' by the Faith and Order Secretariat of the World Council of Churches. I was privileged to be a member of the small Geneva staff working group assigned to assist the editors of *Cantate Domino* during the four years it took to complete the book. The tune CENTRAL by Pablo Sosa of Argentina, is published in *Cantate Domino*.

14 Not so much a hymn (1)

City of man, how rich and right
outspread your streets and squares.
How grand the standards of your life
how high your stocks and shares.

How true the race of life is run:
one holy hard routine;
the sons of God are faring well,
and even death is clean.

City of man, how deep and grim
your camps and shacks and holes.
How wide the eyes of hungry men;
how bitter human souls.

How great the glories of the fight,
the glamour of your wrong.
The sons of God are classified:
some do, some don't belong.

City of God, how broad and far
your walls sublime should spread.
Unharmed and harmless are your ways
and worthy is your creed.

God of the city, God of man,
your church arrest and shake,
to live and lose, to care and feed,
for Christ, whose bread we break.

A bit tongue in cheek, this one (see also No.132). It was obviously suggested by the opening line of Samuel Johnson's (1822 - 82) hymn 'City of God', and originally included as 'Not so much a hymn' in *Pilgrim Praise* to the tune RICHMOND.

15 A hymn for Advent and Christmas 8.7.8.7.D.

Come and be surprised, all nations,
here behold the love divine;
love to still all aspirations:
God concerned with humankind.
Come and see this speechless speaking,
see the Word in human form;
love through every barrier breaking,
love as basis, end and norm.

Come and see how Jesus entered
earthly life, as did we all;
see how kings and workers centred
round this baby in a stall.
See him, who in splendour great is,
for a time in homely care;
see how Christ in humble status
came with us our life to share.

To your holy invitation
we respond, and come, and see.
Kindle our imagination,
that our joy may lasting be.
Jesus, by your coming save us,
by your passion heal our pain;
let no fear nor death enslave us:
by your Easter may we reign!

The opening line owes its inspiration to a Dutch carol 'Komt, verwondert U hier, mensen', but for the rest this text goes very much its own way. Written for the Pilgrim Church in Plymouth in 1963, it appears in *Pilgrim Praise*, where it is suggested to the tune BETHANY by Henry Smart (1813 - 79).

16 Come, dare to be all that you are in Christ

10.5.5.11.

Come, dare to be all that you are in Christ;
be what his loving,
be what his thinking
see in your person: you are eternal light.

All that you have, he gave to you at first;
challenge and courage,
will and commitment,
spring from one fountain: so you will never thirst.

From yoke or bond his love has set you free;
free to love others,
praising and serving
Christ who is present in human lives we see.

Even today you are what you will be;
judged and forgiven,
from death arisen,
take up life's fullness, for Christ has made you free!

This is one of twenty translations of Swedish hymns and songs, commissioned by that grand old man of Swedish hymnody, Anders Frostenson. The booklet *Songs and Hymns from Sweden* was intended to present to the English-speaking world of worship a typical sample of outstanding Swedish texts and tunes of the past fifteen years. The original of this text is by Dr. Frostenson himself, to a melody, TRULY FREE composed by Roland Forsberg.

17 Wind of change

6.5.6.5.D.

Come, O Holy Spirit,
set the church on fire;
strike it as the lightning
hits a reaching spire.
Burn away the structures
and consume the sham
of our holy systems:
Come, in Jesus' name!

Blow away the cobwebs
of our stubborn past.
Come, blow up among us
myths unfit to last.
Wind of change, pursue us
and disturb our calm;
teach us what true love is,
take our hearts by storm.

Cut in us the cackle
of our Babel mind;
spark in us a language
all can understand.
Break into our prison,
come and show us how
all the world lies open:
Pentecost is now!

A text written for a Pentecost service at the ecumenical centre in
Geneva on June 19, 1972, to the tune AU CLAIR DE LA LUNE.
First published in the full music edition of *Pilgrim Praise* in 1972.

18 A hymn on God being for us

Committed to Christ,
who died, but who rose,
we rise in his name,
to trials exposed.
He calls us to serve him
at risk in the crowd.
to do what is right,
even when not allowed.

Hold out to the end
and be not afraid!
He whom we proclaim
will come to our aid.
His Spirit will show us
the truth and the way,
and give us to utter
the things we shall say.

No danger nor death,
no future how grim,
no hatred nor rule
can part us from him
whose promise enfolds us
wherever we move;
for nothing can fetter
the flow of his love.

A straightforward scriptural hymn based on *Matthew 10: 16-26* and *Romans 8: 31-39*, following a casual request by a Dutch Reformed minister in South Africa for a hymn-text on the latter scripture passage. It was first published in *Break Not the Circle*, and has a tune specially composed for it by Doreen Potter. The tune is named CLAUDIUS after the well-known Brazilian architect and cartoonist Claudius Ceccon.

19 A song from those who were there

11 11.11 11.
and chorus 7.7.7.7.D.

Divided by cultures, traditions and speech,
yet one in the Spirit, and caring for each,
we come for the love of the One who creates
our hope of reunion, who frees and unites.
Halleluiah, harambee;
praise the Lord, and join in one.
Maranatha, kyrie;
pray that Jesus will return.
Sing a new Magnificat;
sing that God is great today.
Dance and sing, the news is glad;
halleluiah, harambee!

Together, we look at our lives and confess
our motives of greed, our reluctance to bless,
and pray for new wills to replenish the earth,
that life may be whole, free from hunger and dearth.
Chorus

God's generous presence in human events
redeems us from shelters of selfish defence;
He gives us the courage with others to build
one home for the future: a gentle new world.
Chorus

We come and we go with the Spirit that blows
and, following Jesus wherever he goes,
we revel in Easter, rise up in His name
to fight against powers that stifle and maim.
Chorus

Our coming and going are rhythm and rhyme
for singing and service, for living in time.
Adeste fideles! — and dance into night,
disperse in the city as bearers of light!
Chorus

Hardly a hymn or even a song! It was written at the request of the editor of the *International Review of Mission* for the January 1976 issue (Vol.LXV No.257) of that journal, giving the story of Nairobi, the Fifth Assembly of the World Council of Churches. It is very much a text for insiders, who will recognise in it Swahili words that featured prominently in the Assembly's life; as well as references to specific events during the Assembly, which ended on December 10, in the middle of Advent. Hence the reference to *Adeste Fideles*, a carol sung in the closing service, after the delegates had left the Kenyatta Conference Centre, before they all dispersed into the city. At this stage no one has set it to music.

20 Down-to-earth

6 6 6.6 6.
and chorus 5 5.3 3.6.

Down to earth, as a dove,
came to light holy love:
Jesus Christ from above
  bringing great salvation
  meant for every nation.
  Let us sing, sing, sing,
  Dance and spring, spring, spring,
  Christ is here,
  Ever near!
  Gloria in excelsis.

This is love come to light,
now is fear put to flight.
God defeats darkest night;
  giving for our sorrows
  hope of new tomorrows.
  Chorus

Christ the Lord comes to feed
hungry people in need;
in the house there is bread:
  Jesus in a stable,
  in the church a table.
  Chorus

In verse three, the words remind us that Bethlehem = house of bread.
My fascination with the tune THEODORIC from *Piae Cantiones*
prompted me to write a text that might be usable if ever 'Personent
hodie' went into disuse. The text, apart from appearing in *Pilgrim Praise*
received its first major 'airing' in *The Canadian Hymnbook*. The source
of the melody has not been traced beyond a 1360 gradual; it first
appeared in *Piae Cantiones*, in 1582. American composer
Ron Klusmeier made a new tune for it (Vintage Records SCV 132), as
did Austin Lovelace of Denver, Colorado - the tune, INGWOOD is
included in *Ecumenical Praise*. It appears in *Pilgrim Praise* to a tune
DANCE AND SPRING by I-to Loh.

21 Hymn for a new morning

Each morning with its newborn light
proclaims the Lord of life is great!
His faithfulness will have no end;
to him our songs of praise ascend.

The gift of light that fills the sky
helps us to see and choose our way;
then let us order our affairs
in praise of him who for us cares.

Lord, let our eyes, the body's light,
be drawn to what is good and right
and to yourself, the source of life,
our hope in fear, our peace in strife.

You, Lord of all creation, are
as brilliant as the morning star;
light in our hearts your holy flame
and make us fit to bear your name.

Dispel the darkness from our days
and free us from all bitterness,
from haughty mind and blinded sight,
and lead us forward day and night.

To walk as in the light of day,
be steadfast always, come what may,
we turn in faith to you, our Friend,
and pray: sustain us to the end.

Translated for the fourth edition of *Cantate Domino* from a German original by Johannes Zwick (1496 - 1542) to a melody written in 1537 by Johann Walter for the well-known German hymn 'Vom Himmel Hoch'. A slightly later tune (1539) attributed to Martin Luther is unfortunately also known as VOM HIMMEL HOCH (see *Hymns and Psalms*, No.100).

22 'Today is the first day of the rest of your life'

8 10. 8 4.

Each Sunday brings to mind again
that Jesus is risen, the Easterman;
that life has never been the same
since Eastertime.

The sign of every rising sun,
the thought of the life in the grave begun,
renews our will to do and dare
and clears the air.

Each Sunday sets the tone anew
for labour and leisure the whole week through;
for Easter turns the dullest day
to holy play.

Of all our days that still remain,
to-day is the first, let us rise again
and run with haste to spread the word:
'We've seen the Lord!'

Each Sunday is the starting point
for freedom in which we are called to join
the movement that will lead to change
till love shall reign.

This text was written during the second Synod of the Church of North India, in New Delhi in July 1974, and was sparked off by a casual remark by someone from the floor of a plenary session. It was included in *Break Not the Circle* to a tune LANNAMAN by Doreen Potter.

23 A hymn of homelessness

10 10. 10 10.

Each year we sing with bated Christmas voice,
as if events in Bethlehem were nice;
when every house and pub had shut its door,
and Mary in a shed her baby bore.

Forgive us, Lord, that things are still the same,
that Christ is homeless under other names;
still holy fam'lies to our cities come,
where life is sick and sore in crowded slum.

Lord, make it clear that joy will be denied,
unless the door into our life stands wide;
that even with our tables richly spread,
our house of life is short of living bread.

Give us, O Father, restlessness of soul,
till right is done and life is healed and whole;
keep us impatient till the time has come,
when all your children are on earth at home.

Entitled 'A hymn for Shelter', this text was written for the Housing
Action Group 'Shelter' during the year when I was closely involved
in the setting up of the Plymouth branch of that organisation
(1965). It is included in *Pilgrim Praise* under the title 'A hymn of
homelessness' to a traditional tune FARLEY CASTLE by Henry Lawes
(1596 - 1662) and to a contemporary tune OLIVE specially composed
for this text by Doreen Potter.

24 Earth is shaken to its bed-rock

8.10.9.9.

Earth is shaken to its bed-rock.
Like a straw our confidence is broken.
His unequalled might rules creation;
facing God with God our only hope.

He alone can bring us all things
more and closer still than air and water,
penetrating all. Why go seeking
him whose being fills, embraces all?

All we have to do is trust him,
willing nothing but his will and purpose,
and his constant love, strong, persuasive,
seeking out, and finding, all who live.

A translation from Swedish of an Arthur Lundkvist and Anders
Frostenson text. They wrote it following the earthquake in Agadir,
Morocco, in 1961. The music EARTH IS SHAKEN in *Songs and
Hymns from Sweden* is by Sven-Eric Johanson.

25 Establish, Lord, your kingdom

7.6.7.6.6.

Establish, Lord, your kingdom;
map out for us the way
where even in the darkness
our feet will never stray.
Lord, you make all things new.

We hail each dawn of promise,
that rises with the sun,
as if it were your first day,
our first and only one.
Lord, you make all things new.

Give words, unheard, unspoken,
to fill our heart with song,
and teach us how to worship
with hands and feet and tongue.
Lord, you make all things new.

The world of fern and insect,
of fossil, gem and stone,
it links us with creation,
before our life began.
Lord, you make all things new.

From loneliness redeem us
and help us be at home
in your created order;
O come, Lord Jesus, come,
for you make all things new.

Translation of an Anders Frostenson text, to a melody ALL THINGS NOW by Roland Forsberg in *Songs and Hymns from Sweden*. Frostenson identifies *Revelation 21: 5* and *Matthew 6: 10* as biblical references.

26 Faith, while trees are still in blossom

8.7.8.7.

Faith, while trees are still in blossom,
plans the picking of the fruit;
faith can feel the thrill of harvest,
when the buds begin to sprout.

Long before the dawn is breaking,
faith anticipates the sun.
Faith is eager for the daylight,
for the work that must be done.

Long before the rains were coming,
Noah went and built an ark.
Abraham, the lonely migrant,
saw the Light beyond the dark.

Faith, uplifted, tamed the water
of the undivided sea
and the people of the Hebrews
found the path that made them free.

Faith believes that God is faithful,
– He will be who He will be –
Faith accepts his call, responding:
'I am willing; Lord, send me'.

Another Frostenson lyric, with biblical references as *John 4: 35; John 5: 56; Hebrews 11: 1* and *Isaiah 5: 6*. Ron Klusmeier (USA) also wrote a new tune for it (Praise Records, Canada, PRS 369), as did American composer Alec Wyton, who wrote the tune FAITH especially for *Ecumenical Praise*. In *Songs and Hymns from Sweden* the Gustaf Bjarnegard melody TREES IN BLOSSOM is used.

27 A hymn on work and worship   6.5.6.5.D.

Father, help your people
in this world to build
something of your kingdom,
and to do your will.
Lead us to discover
partnership in love;
bless our ways of sharing,
and our pride reprove.

Lord of desk and altar,
bind our lives in one,
that in work and worship
love may set the tone.
Give us grace to listen,
clarity of speech;
make us truly thankful
for the gifts of each.

Holy is the setting
of each room and yard,
lecture hall and kitchen,
office, shop and ward.
Holy is the rhythm
of our working hours;
hallow then our purpose,
energy and powers.

Strengthen, Lord, for service,
hand and heart and brain;
help us good relations
daily to maintain.
Let the living presence
of the servant-Christ
heighten our devotion,
make our life a feast.

The occasion for writing this text was a worship event at the ecumenical centre on Monday, June 8, 1970. Staff members of organisations that have their headquarters in the Geneva ecumenical centre start the week on Monday mornings with a half-hour act of worship in which the various church traditions represented in the centre are reflected, from traditional orthodox to experimental 'free' church.

The theme for this particular Monday was Berthold Brecht's 'Fragen eines lesenden Arbeiters' - Questions from a reading worker. Originally, this hymn contained phrases that were much more closely related to the life in 'the house' (as the ecumenical centre is affectionately called) than is the case in the present revised version. Verse 1 originally went like this: 'Father, help your people in this *house* to build . . .' Verse 3 in its original version read:

> Holy is the setting
> of each wing and floor,
> meeting room and kitchen,
> cyclostyle and store . . .

We sang it to AU CLAIR DE LA LUNE, but Robin Sheldon, editor of the Anglican Hymnbook wrote a melody to which this text was sung in a May 1973 'Come and Sing' event in the Westminster Abbey, when I was asked to introduce a programme of hymns from *Pilgrim Praise*.

28 The life of our time

11.10.11.10.

Father, we long to be people more human
and to be part of a world more humane;
we want to be like the Man whom you gave us,
freed by his love and to service ordained.

Lord, let your Spirit reprove calm and caution,
all that is dull from our spirits remove.
Fire our concern for the world and the nations,
take us to take to your children your love.

Father, we long for your reign in our lifetime:
freedom from hunger and hatred and shame,
peace for all people and bread on each table;
save us from wasting the life of our time.

Written especially for the full music edition of *Pilgrim Praise*, this hymn has been set to two different tunes: WOBURN WALK by Christopher Bowers-Broadbent, and HUMAN TIME by Patrick Routley. In the original draft of this text, I had LIEBSTER IMMANUEL in mind, in J. S. Bach's arrangement (from *Himmels-Lust*, 1679).

29 A hymn for after the communion (1)

8 8 8.7.

Father, who in Jesus found us,
God, whose love is all around us,
who to freedom new unbound us,
  keep our hearts with joy aflame.

For the sacramental breaking,
for the honour of partaking,
for your life our lives re-making,
  young and old, we praise your name.

From the service of this table
lead us to a life more stable
for our witness make us able;
  blessings on our work we claim.

Through our calling closely knitted,
daily to your praise committed,
for a life of service fitted,
  let us now your love proclaim.

Among the earlier hymns I wrote for the Pilgrim Church in Plymouth, there were several related to the church's celebration of the sacraments of baptism and holy communion. This text was written in 1965 with the melody QUEM PASTORES LAUDAVERE in mind (14th century German). H. W. Holmsen was commissioned to compose a new tune AFLAME to appear in *Pilgrim Praise*.

30 Living no longer for ourselves

8.7.8.7.7 7.

For ourselves no longer living,
let us live for Christ alone;
of ourselves more strongly giving,
go as far as he has gone:
    Son of God who chose to be
    Son of Man to set us free.

If we are to live for others,
share as equals human worth,
join the round of sisters, brothers,
that encircles all the earth!
    All the fullness earth affords,
    is the people's, is the Lord's.

Fighting fear and exploitation
is our daily common call;
finding selfhood, building nations,
sharing what we have with all.
    As the birds that soar in flight,
    let us rise and face the light.

Let us rise and join the forces
that combine to do God's will,
wisely using earth's resources,
human energy and skill.
    Let us *now*, by love released,
    celebrate the future's feast!

I wrote this during the Lusaka Assembly of the All Africa Conference of Churches in May 1974. I was inspired by the theme of the Assembly, which was in turn related to *2 Corinthians 5: 15*. It appears in *Break Not the Circle* to the only tune I have ever composed. As I cannot even read music, it was necessary to ask Doreen Potter to harmonise it! The name of the tune, TUCKSTONE, is a tribute to the late Dr. Tommy Tucker and to Mrs. Tucker, of Livingstone, who were my gracious hosts in Zambia, and generous ministers of encouragement to me in my work as a hymnwriter.

31 Seven is sufficient

6.5.6.5.

For the crowd of thousands
sitting on the ground,
seven is sufficient,[1]
seven will go round.[2]

Seven is sufficient,
fish and loaves of bread,[3]
Jesus, for our hunger,
gives us life instead.

Jesus makes his offer:
fish and bread as food,
Make us truly thankful,[4]
make our living good.

If we give to Jesus
bread to bless and break,
five and two will feed us
seven days a week.

What we give to Jesus,
and with others share,
will at last be gathered:
'over and to spare'!

[1] *Seven symbolizes fullness.*
[2] *Go round - circle round a table stands for fellowship*
[3] *Fish (Ichthys), Greek for Jesus Christ, Son of God, Saviour*
   Bread = Christ = bread of the world
[4] *From a well-known grace*

Dr. Willem Barnard, one of Holland's leading poet-theologians, is the author of the original Dutch text on which this paraphrase is based. It was sung at the Pilgrim Church in Plymouth to GLENFINLAS by Kenneth George Finlay (1882) but in *Pilgrim Praise* it appears with CASWALL by F. Filitz (1804 - 76).

32 A hymn of human rights

8.7.8.7.8.7.

For the healing of the nations,
Lord, we pray with one accord;
for a just and equal sharing
of the things that earth affords.
To a life of love in action
help us rise and pledge our word.

Lead us, Father, into freedom,
from despair your world release;
that redeemed from war and hatred,
all may come and go in peace.
Show us how through care and goodness
fear will die and hope increase.

All that kills abundant living,
let it from the earth be banned;
pride of status, race or schooling,
dogmas that obscure your plan.
In our common quest for justice
may we hallow life's brief span.

You, creator-God, have written
your great name on humankind;
for our growing in your likeness
bring the life of Christ to mind;
that by our response and service
earth its destiny may find.

Of all the hymns I have written, this is the text that has been more widely reprinted and incorporated in major hymnbooks than any other. It was first used in 1965 in a worship service at the Pilgrim Church, Plymouth, to mark Human Rights Day (December 10). Subsequently, it has been used on many official occasions, such as the 25th anniversary of the United Nations Organisation in St. Pierre Cathedral, Geneva, and the 50th anniversary of the International Labour Organisation, also in Geneva. When introduced in a 'Come and Sing' lecture at the Westminster Abbey, London, 1973, it was sung to Henry Purcell's WESTMINSTER ABBEY with which it has been principally associated ever since.

In 1983 this text, together with words from the Latin Missal: 'Pacem relinquo vobis, pacem meam do vobis, etc. . .', was set to music by the contemporary Norwegian composer Knut Nystedt. The cantata, commissioned by the United Church of Christ in DesMoines, USA, received its European première in Uppsala Cathedral in June 1983.

It appears in *Pilgrim Praise* to PICARDY and the *Hymnal Supplement* to a tune by Carl Schalk, FORTUNATUS NEW.

The fourth line of verse 3 originally read 'dogmas keeping man from man'.

33 A hymn for an international act of worship

8.7.8.7.7 7.

Gathered here from many nations,
one in worship and intent,
let us for the days that face us
all our hopes to God present,
    that our life and work may be
    full of joy and truly free.

May the spring of all our actions
be, O Lord, your love for man;
may your word be seen and spoken
and your will be clearly done.
    Help us, who your image bear,
    for the good of each to care.

Give us grace to match our calling,
faith to overcome the past;
show us how to meet the future,
planning boldly, acting fast.
    Let the servant-mind of Christ
    in our life be manifest.

Now ourselves anew committing
to each other and to you,
Lord, we ask that you will train us
for the truth we have to do;
    that the world may soon become
    your great city of shalom.

This hymn was written for ecumenical/international worship events, and had its origin in Monday worship at the Geneva ecumenical centre. Written in 1971, it was first publicly used at the 1972 meeting of the World Council of Churches' Central Committee in Utrecht, the Netherlands. The melody KINGSTON with which it appears in *Cantate Domino* was specially composed for this text by Jamaican composer Doreen Potter (1925 - 80). The last word of the text is a striking use of the Hebrew 'Shalom' to speak of a city of peace.

34 Glory and anguish

10 10.10 10.
(Dactyllic)

Glory and anguish to God in the height,
peace and goodwill and disaster and fright;
angels and orphans discordantly cry:
Glory to God in the depth of the day.

Father almighty and powerless Lord,
whose word is our healing, whose love is our hurt,
from you we escape and to you we belong;
we have your praise on the tip of our tongue.

Help us your glory on earth to discern
and to discover where Christ is re-born;
prompt us his presence in people to name,
heaven and earth are united in him.

© 1972 Hope Publishing Company for USA and Canada and Stainer & Bell Ltd
for other territories

Not quite a straightforward Gloria, written as a 'companion piece' to
'Lord, do not hold yourself apart' (Kyrie), for the 1972 full music
edition of *Pilgrim Praise*. QUEDLINBURG was originally suggested
as a tune (J. C. Kittel, 1732 - 1809), but in *Pilgrim Praise*, DELHI
(E. F. Rimbault, 1816 - 76) is given as an alternative.

35 Glory to God in the highest

8.7.7.8.
with alleluiahs

Glory to God in the highest,
where none tramples other down,
where people practise loving;
glory to God among people.
Alleluiah, alleluiah

Glory to God in the highest,
where none lifts an angry fist,
where peace is strongly fought for;
glory to God among people.
Chorus

Glory to God in the highest,
where someone abandons self,
where people share with others;
glory to God among people.
Chorus

During the Nairobi Assembly of the World Council of Churches, Peter Janssens and his 'Song Orchestra' needed an English translation of a Hans-Jürgen Netz song (and fast!). 'Glory to God in the highest' was the result. The melody EHRE SEI GOTT for it is by Peter Janssens himself. The song is included on the LP *Break down the walls* (Pietbiet Records 1024).

36 God calls his people

D.C.M.

God calls his people firm to stand,
with them his work is shared.
To follow Christ with open mind
let Christians be prepared.
We know that they who venture much
will master earthly strife,
and they who give and spend themselves
will gain a fuller life.

God calls, and he provides the grace
to undergird our will;
it gives us confidence that he
can good create from ill.
Beyond each barrier that divides
he shows the vision clear
of new creative human-ness
in every field and sphere.

God calls, and powers that break and part
are void; and all are one,
united in a life of love
together with his Son.
Whate'er across the world may rage,
yet wins his purpose through,
and in each Christ-belonging heart
his reign begins anew!

A translation of a Jan Jacob Thomson (1882 - 1961) Dutch original.
I wrote the English translation for the farewell service I conducted in
my first pastorate in Barry, South Wales, before moving to the Pilgrim
Church in Plymouth. The tune to which this hymn has always been
sung in Dutch churches is ELLACOMBE (*Mainz Gesangbuch,* 1833),
and is in *Pilgrim Praise.*

37 A hymn on Galatians 3:16–22 11.10.11.10.

God calls us to the fellowship of living!
Heaven exceeds the things we understand,
and here below our feet are firmly planted
on the good earth, our greening motherland.

God is our future, God is Lord and Father,
who causes on our days his light to shine,
whose grace has kept our earthy world together;
he gave us space, he gives the span of time.

The Word he gave to Abraham, our father,
came as a seed to blossom in his seed,
ready to face the times that are approaching,
when the great harvest ripens on the field.

Yes, we are sons and daughters of the promise,
the children of the day that is to come,
when he, the Son, the Sun, descends proclaiming
his peace and justice to each human home.

A translation of Willem Barnard's Dutch text: 'Mensen, wij zijn
geroepen om te leven!', based on *Galatians 3: 16-22*, the epistle reading
for the 13th Sunday after Pentecost. The translation was especially
commissioned for the closing service of the 1972 World Council of
Churches' Central Committee meeting in the large Domcathedral in
Utrecht. It is usually sung to Loys Bourgeois' PSALM 12.

38 The rape of the land

L.M.

God gave us as in trust to hold
creation and its wealth untold,
but we have with uncaring hand
destroyed its green and raped the land.

We strip the trees and leave them bare,
pollute the streams, the soil, the air,
and we have never truly faced
the outcome of our ways of waste.

But now, with millions underfed,
and poison in our daily bread,
we view creation with alarm:
is there still time to heal the harm?

May God forgive the curse of greed,
alert our mind to human need,
that we again may purify
the life of earth and sea and sky.

Entitled 'The rape of the land', this hymn sings of the way in which earth is plundered, and people fail to re-plenish it. I-to Loh (Taiwan) composed a tune, CONSERVATION, and included the hymn in *New Songs of Asian Cities*. In the 1972 edition of *Pilgrim Praise* the text appears to BRESLAU from *As Hymnodus Sacer*, Leipzig, 1625; and to a new melody DROXFORD specially written by Peter Tranchell. The original first line of the hymn in *Pilgrim Praise* was: 'God gave to man, to have and hold'.

39 A hymn on freedom (with etymological interruptions)

8.7.8.7.
and chorus 6.6.6.6.

Freedom is to people
what air is to the birds.
Freedom is belonging,
breaking bread, sharing words.

God has set us free for freedom,
for responding 'yes' or 'no'.
Freedom is his gift and calling,
he has let his people go.

free - Sanskrit priyas: dear, belonging, as members
of a household connected by ties of kindred with
the head, as opposed to slaves.

Ties of kindred are our bondage:
we the members, he the head.
God has made us in his image;
love has made us free indeed.

free - Old English freon, Gothic frijon: to love, Old
High German friunt: friend. German freien, Dutch
vrijen: to court, make love.

God unties our hands for loving
man or woman, children, friends,
caring for the other's wholeness;
love is kind and understands.

free - German frei, related to Friede, meaning peace,
reconciliation; zufrieden: content.

Human hearts remain in turmoil
till they find their rest in God.
He is source of peace and freedom,
gives us Christ in flesh and blood.

Give us freedom, Lord, to serve you,
show us where we ought to go,
never resting till all people's
cups are full and overflow.

Something of a hymnological oddity, this text, in that it has etymological interruptions. The associated meanings and connotations of the word 'free' are so rich that they give scope for a widely varied text on the subject. Written originally for *Break Not the Circle* with music EMANCIPATION by Doreen Potter, this text was also given a different melody by Ron Klusmeier (USA) who included it in a two-record album *Ron and Kris and Fred and Walter* (Kari Records, Canada, KRK 10375).

40 God in the midst

6.6.6.6.8 8.

God is unique and one —
Father, Sustainer, Lord!
Patterns of life were spun
by his creative Word.
Of his intention, love and care
we are with growing trust aware.

Love came to earth in Christ,
our common life to share;
choosing to be the least,
willing a cross to bear.
He died, he rose, that we might live
and all our love, responding, give.

The Holy Spirit moves
man to discover man;
his inspiration proves
more than the mind can span.
Each listening heart is led to find
the will of God for all mankind.

He shall forever reign,
ruler of time and space;
God in the midst of life,
seen in the human face.
We give expression to our creed
by love in thought, in word and deed.

I had always wanted a new text for Martin Shaw's exciting 1915 tune LITTLE CORNARD. Inspiration came when I was looking for a credal hymn for use in worship at the Pilgrim Church, Plymouth. Stanley L. Osborne, secretary of the Canadian Hymnbook Committee wrote in his book . . . *if such holy song*: 'these stanzas are, as it were, a little sermon, and for that reason it makes good sense when the congregation reads them as a postscript to the sermon'. The title of the hymn in *Pilgrim Praise* is 'God in the midst'. Titles for my hymns are usually carefully chosen.

41 A hymn (?) on God being unfair—thank God

8.8.8.8.8.8.

God makes his rain to fall, his sun
to shine alike on good and bad.   *Matthew 5: 45*
A father takes his wastrel son
to heart as risen from the dead,
while he who never disobeyed
rejects the music, stays outside.   *Luke 15: 11 - 32*

A shepherd leaves his faithful flock
to search for one who strays away.   *Matthew 18: 12*
To workers hired at five o'clock
and those who toiled the length of day
the owner of the vineyard pays
unequal work with equal wage.   *Matthew 20: 1 - 16*

A thief is promised paradise!   *Luke 23: 43*
The mean are helped to start again.   *Luke 19: 1 - 10*
God is not fair to us in Christ;
he takes away our guilt and sin.
God is not fair the way we are;
his thoughts outweigh our thoughts by far.

As I wrote under No.**40**, titles of my hymns are usually carefully chosen. No.**41** proves that point in that the title of this text is 'A hymn (?) on God being unfair - thank God'. It sings of all those occasions in the Gospels where God's ways turn out to be higher than our ways. Biblical references are given in the margin with the hymn. Jamaican composer Doreen Potter wrote two melodies for it in *Break Not the Circle*, entitled - not untypically - GRACE and CARITAS.

42 A hymn on God filling all in all

8.7.8.7.
and chorus 8 8.6.

God of bible and tradition,
of experience and church,
whom we worship and petition,
home and joy of human search:
Give us faith to see you clearly,
love you dearly, follow nearly,
every day, all the way.

God of white and greening mountain,
rising forest, hazy height;
Lord of sea and sky enchanting,
colour, fragrance, music, light:
Chorus

God, who brought to birth from water
all the things that grow and move;
Lord of all created order,
God in lamb and fish and dove;
Chorus

God in people, rich and dying,
God in mansion, ghetto, slum;
heard in silence and in crying,
shared in bread and stolen crumb:
Chorus

God in Christ, with human features,
God in Jesus for all time,
coming down to free us, teach us,
God of destiny and name:
Chorus

This hymn was triggered off in my mind when I attended the 1974 meeting of the European Area of the World Alliance of Reformed Churches, held in Frankfurt in September. Under the general theme 'Criteria of theological truth', Professor D. W. D. Shaw gave a paper on 'Scripture, tradition and experience'. As I listened to his lecture, my mind kept wandering off, and I was able to write this text down fairly quickly after the meeting. The refrain is based on a prayer by St. Richard of Chichester. The tune, composed for it by Doreen Potter, entitled ST. LUCIA appears in *Break Not the Circle*.

43 God's kingdom is among us

7.6.7.6.

God's kingdom is among us,
not vague and far away,
no fairy tale or fancy;
his kingdom is today!

God meets us in the city,
in ambulance and fear,
in flashing light and siren
and in the surgeon's care.

His kingdom is in churches,
at home and in hotels,
in hospitals and prisons
and at conveyor belts.

Then let us trace the kingdom;
its rule is never far:
God's kingdom simply happens
wherever people are!

Translation from Swedish of a text by the eminent poet Bo Setterlind, written in 1967: 'Guds rike är ej fjärran'. Biblical reference for verse 1 is given as *Luke 17: 21*. The translation was done, together with nineteen others, for the collection *Songs and Hymns from Sweden*. The melody GOD EVERYWHERE was composed for this text by Karl-Olof Robertson (1974).

44 The daughter of Jairus

7.6.7.6.

God's word throughout the ages
has been the source of life,
and still it raises people
out of their tomb of grief.

The house was full of sadness;
a little girl had died.
Her father ran to Jesus
and like a man he cried.

He pleaded for his daughter
before the Son of man:
Lord, lay your hand upon her
and she will live again.

The house was full of mourners,
the street was dark with gloom,
when Jesus came and entered
the stillness of her room.

He touched her with his speaking
and took her by the hand;
he gave the girl her Easter
and helped her live and stand.

He gave the mourners laughter;
the girl another chance.
He stopped the sad procession
by leading death a dance.

Your church is like a daughter
who oversleeps in death;
Lord, touch her with your spirit
and bring her back to life.

Another text by Dr. Willem Barnard, translated from the Dutch. It is a paraphrase of a song about the daughter of Jairus. In *Pilgrim Praise* it is given with two tunes: EWING (Alexander Ewing, 1830 - 95); and a new melody AWAKENING specially composed by H. W. Holmsen. In North America, Ron Klusmeier wrote yet another tune for this text, and included it in an LP *Song circling all the earth* (Praise Records PRS 369). In October 1976, in St. David's United Church of Canada, Calgary, this hymn was sung by Kris Klusmeier at a sing-along concert, while, for the first time ever, it was expressed in dance by Gayda Errett.

45 We must evolve it

God the narrator,
logically speaking,
in the beginning
shaped the good earth.
    Out of his true love,
    speaking-and-do-love,
    blossomed and grew love;
    life came to birth.

God the beginning
spoke and created
life in his image,
people alive.
    Born to subdue-love,
    care-and-pursue-love,
    make-and-speak-true-love,
    born to survive.

This is the sequel
of the narration:
we must evolve it
to the good end,
    drawing on do-love,
    every-day-new-love,
    seeing-it-through-love,
    peace to extend.

Written in 1972 to that mesmerising old Gaelic tune BUNESSAN. The text 'plays around' with the idea that the Hebrew 'dabar' signifies word as well as deed, and that the opening lines of John's Gospel (In the beginning was the Word - logos) has logical consequences: whenever God speaks, things happen. In *Pilgrim Praise* a new tune ST. PANCRAS was written for it by Christopher Bowers-Broadbent.

46 The first and final word

8.7.8.7.8.7.

God who spoke in the beginning,
forming rock and shaping spar,
set all life and growth in motion,
earthly world and distant star;
he who calls the earth to order
is the ground of what we are.

God who spoke through people, nations,
through events long past and gone,
showing still today his purpose,
speaks supremely through his Son;
he who calls the earth to order
gives his word and it is done.

God whose speech becomes incarnate
— Christ is servant, Christ is Lord! —
calls us to a life of service,
heart and will to action stirred;
he who uses our obedience
has the first and final word.

The message of this hymn is much along the same lines as that of the previous text. *Cf. Psalm 33: 9*: 'For he spoke and it was; he commanded and it stood firm'. One of the most important phrases in the King James version of the Bible - now lost in the more modern translations - was 'and it came to pass that . . .' The melody for this text, CORBRIDGE was written for it by Erik Routley, for the fourth edition of *Cantate Domino*.

47 Hosanna from the paving stones   8.7.8.7.8.7 7.

God will, when he comes down to earth,
have little ground for laughter;
he'll find the Christians cold and slack,
content with arch and rafter.
But he is there for everyone,
his thought is with the lowly,
not only with the holy.

That's why the churches are too small,
where hymns are sung on Sunday.
With Christ alive, the very streets
will shout for joy on Monday!
Hosanna from the paving stones,
and from the congregation!
– He knows our meditation –.

God will, when he comes down to earth,
have little ground for laughter;
again we nail him to the cross
and go to war and slaughter.
But even silence spells our guilt
in churches and in cities.
Pray God that he has pity!

That's why the churches are too small
with singing congregations:
the world itself must be the stage
for workday celebrations.
It starts when people see with fright
their loveless ways of living.
God knows, we need forgiving.

There will, when God comes down to earth,
be only ground for laughter
with those who leave their selfish game
and join to follow after
the God who teaches us the round
from worship on the Sunday
to service on the Monday.

A translation, specially written for *Cantate Domino* of Dieter Trautwein's 1964 hymn 'Kommt Gott als Mensch in Dorf und Stadt'. It appears to a tune PALMSONNTAG written in that year by Gottfried Neubert and a group attending a music workshop. 'Hosanna from the paving stones' (verse 2) is directly related to *Luke 19: 40*.

48 A hymn on acceptance

7.6.7.6.D.

Help us accept each other
as Christ accepted us;
teach us as sister, brother,
each person to embrace.
Be present, Lord, among us
and bring us to believe
we are *ourselves* accepted
and meant to love and live.

Teach us, O Lord, your lessons,
as in our daily life
we struggle to be human
and search for hope and faith.
Teach us to care for people,
for all — not just for some,
to love them as we find them
or as they may become.

Let your acceptance change us,
so that we may be moved
in living situations
to do the truth in love;
to practise your acceptance
until we know by heart
the table of forgiveness
and laughter's healing art.

Lord, for today's encounters
with all who are in need,
who hunger for acceptance,
for righteousness and bread,
we need new eyes for seeing,
new hands for holding on:
renew us with your Spirit;
Lord, free us, make us one!

This text was set in motion upon reading a Bible study article Mrs. Jackie Mattonen had written for the Cumberland Presbyterian Church in the USA. Mrs. Mattonen was for several years a member of the Executive Committee of the World Alliance of Reformed Churches on the staff of which I served from 1968 until 1978. The melody BARONITA was composed especially by Doreen Potter for *Break Not the Circle*. It has become very popular in the USA to a tune ACCEPTANCE by John Ness Beck. It was almost accidentally and at the last moment included in the fourth edition of *Cantate Domino*, when the editors were forced to drop a particular text for which the author asked an exorbitant copyright fee, and it so happened that my 'Hymn on acceptance' was just of the right length to fill the two blank pages that needed filling. It appeared there with a German and Dutch translation which had been written especially for this last minute inclusion. The hymn was also used in the order of service for the 1983 Women's World Day of Prayer.

Bible reference for verse 1, line 2 is *Romans 15: 7*. The reference for verse 3, line 4 is *John 3: 21* (A.V.) and *Ephesians 4: 15*. For verse 3, line 7 the reference is *Matthew 18: 21*.

49 An Easter song

9.8.9.8.D.

He's back in the land of the living,
the Man we decided to kill;
he's standing among us, forgiving
our guilt of the Good-Friday-hill.
He calls us to share in his rising,
to abandon the grave of our past;
he offers us present and future,
a world that is open and vast.

He's back in a world where the living
are robbing each other of joy,
where people for gain and destruction
the powers of nature employ.
From lofty respectable motives
are crosses erected today,
for people put people on trial
and evil is having its way.

But crosses are also the symbols
of love that is given and spent;
the signs of our hope and survival,
of Easter defeating our Lent.
Through people of passion, responding
to rise against hunger and hell,
new life shall arise from the ashes
of hatred, and all shall be well!

Not so much a hymn as a folksong about the Easter happening. Written for the Pilgrim Church in 1965 to the tune ST. SULIEN (Edward Arthur, 1874 - 1948). In the 1972 full music edition of *Pilgrim Praise* it appears to a new tune NEW LIFE by Michael Metcalf (commissioned by Stainer & Bell Ltd), but probably the most catchy and appropriate musical version is that provided by Ron Klusmeier (USA), who included it on the LP *Thank you that now is the time of our life* (Vintage Records SCV 132, 1973).

50 How can creation's voice be still

C.M.

How can creation's voice be still,
when with us dwells the Word?
A song of praise is raised from earth;
faith rises like a bird.

God dwells as much in grass and dust,
in human souls weighed down,
as in the realm of majesty,
the heavens and their span.

The shepherd's voice is heard to call
through voices that are stilled.
The flock is led in danger's face
but shall not come to ill.

The stone is rolled away; the tomb
becomes the gate of life.
The earth is warmed by tongues of fire
that speak, and none is deaf.

The Word is with us, and the world
is full of light and life.
Lord, give us faithfulness and faith,
alert and seeing eyes.

Translation from the Swedish of an Anders Frostenson text, made for inclusion in *Songs and Hymns from Sweden*. Biblical references given are: verse 1, *John 1: 14;* verse 2, *Isaiah 57: 15;* verse 3, *Mark 16: 18* and *John 10: 27*. The tune with which the original Swedish 1962 text has been associated is Carl Nielsen's CREATION'S VOICE composed in 1919.

51 An Easter carol

How many fruits we gain,
by Jesus' dying proffered,
when he his life in pain
upon the tree had offered.
Yet would our gain be small
and vain his costly giving
if, after losing all,
Christ Jesus was not living.

How barren life would be;
how fruitless our devotion,
when all the guilt we feel
is deeper than the ocean.
How could the human race
endure this burden longer,
had not in evil's face
Christ proved to be the stronger.

Unsure would be our way
and dismal every morning,
were't not that every day
begins like Easter's dawning.
we are on earth at home,
redeemed from sin and crying,
for Jesus has become
the first-fruits from the dying.

The world of nature shows
that life must have an ending;
a nobler being grows
from death to life ascending.
This lesson can be read
in planting seed, and sowing,
in grain that grows for bread:
praise God for all we owe him!

His word invites and wakes
to death and self-denial;
us by the hand he takes
beyond defeat and trial.
Let every life be free
from all that would enslave it,
for risen again is he
who came to earth to save it.

Intrigued by the title VRUECHTEN of the Easter carol melody 'This Joyful Eastertide' I tracked down the original Dutch text of this 17th century piece and translated it into English in 1966. I have tried to remain as close and faithful to the original as possible. The carol dates from 1684. In *Pilgrim Praise*, TABITHA by Christopher Bowers-Broadbent and VRUECHTEN can be found with this text.

52 Psalm 92

7.6 6.7.D.

How wide is life for living,
come, people, raise your song
and let your praise be strong;
God's love is ours for giving.
Proclaim him in the morning,
declare him every night!
His deeds can put to flight
our fears, our tears, our mourning.

The rich who thwart, oppose him
will not achieve their aim.
The Lord will put his name
on those who love and choose him:
he will exalt the humble,
raise up the weak and poor;
he will make strong and sure
the feet of those who stumble.

Lift high your heads and flourish
like cedars rising up,
like palm-trees drawing sap
from streams that flow and nourish.
The Lord is our salvation,
in whom our lives rejoice
with instrument and voice
and daily celebration.

This very free paraphrase of Psalm 92 was inspired by a similar (and
even more free) paraphrase in French written by Henri Künzler of
Geneva who was for several years pastor of the Meyrin congregation
of which I was a member from 1968 - 75. It is sung to the melody to
which it was originally sung in the *Genevan Psalter* of 1562, but in
Break Not the Circle it appears in a new harmonisation by Doreen
Potter. She named the tune MEYRIN.

53 Psalm 23

10 10.10 10.

I can on God implicitly rely;
he stands in all events my person by.
It's he whose love into my prison breaks,
who leads me out and makes my soul relax.

Though I may go through nights of dark despair
and reach the very depth of thoughts that scare,
not even then will I give in to fear
for I am still convinced the Lord is near.

With all my heart I put my trust in God;
he wills for all his people what is good.
Wherever I may go, he too will come
and make me in his presence feel at home.

A paraphrase of Psalm 23 in which I have deliberately tried to avoid using the rural imagery of the shepherd. The name of the tune by Doreen Potter, STREBOHN in *Break Not the Circle*, is a part-anagram of John Roberts, a psychiatrist who for a short time served on the staff of the World Council of Churches. In *Pilgrim Praise* an Alan Ridout tune DENFORD is set to this text.

54 Come to your senses

If you have ears, then listen
to what the Spirit says
and give an open hearing
to wonder and surprise.

If you have eyes for seeing
the word in human form,
then let your love be telling
and your compassion warm.

If you have buds for tasting
the apple of God's eye,
then go, enjoy creation
and people on the way.

If you have hands for caring,
then pray that you may know
the tender art of loving
our world of touch and go.

If you can smell the perfume
of life, the feast of earth,
then sow the seeds of laughter
and tend the shoots of mirth.

Come, people, to your senses
and celebrate the day!
For God gives wine for water
the gift of light for grey.

I wrote this text for Epiphany Sunday in 1970, for an experimental worship service in the Church of Scotland congregation in Geneva. It is a plea to worshipping Christians to get away from the concept that we are hearers of the Word only, and fully to use all the senses God has given us to love him and enjoy him forever. The biblical reference in the last verse is to the story of the wedding in Cana, where Christ changed the colourlessness of water into the sparkle of wine. In *Pilgrim Praise* it appears to a 1588 French dancing treatise, BELLE QUI TIENT MA VIE, but when I introduced it in one of the 1973 'Come and Sing' lectures at Westminster Abbey (organised every month of May by the Hymn Society of Great Britain and Ireland), we sang it to a slightly amended version of the CHERRY TREE CAROL. In *Ecumenical Praise* it is given a fascinating new musical treatment by the American composer Alec Wyton, who called his tune LISTEN.

55 I look for the city

11.9.11.8 8.

I look for the city, I look for a street,
I search for the rivers that widen,
a street and a square and a city that's ours,
belonging to all and to me,
belonging to all and to me.

The street and the square and the city are God's.
He lives, has his being among us;
creation belongs to mankind and to him,
there's nothing that does not belong,
there's nothing that does not belong.

I dream, but I search for the dream that is God's,
which is in our deepest reflected.
The street that disowns us will be his domain,
and Jesus, our brother, is there,
and Jesus, our brother, is there.

A translation from the Swedish of a 1969 text by Anders Frostenson
for which Bertil Hallin wrote the music OUR CITY.

56 A hymn of first, last and in-between

In the beginning: God!
No earth or sea or skies.
In the beginning: God,
but nothing other-wise.
In the beginning: Word,
unheard and still unseen;
not even brooding bird,
no space or time for scene.

When all is said and done,
(in the beginning: God!)
when earth has been and gone,
there will be only God.
He is the first and last,
the seed and sum of life;
there will be no more thirst,
no crying, pain or death.

But for the great between,
unending, unbegun,
the things that can't be seen
He names and they are done.
He gives the human race
its likelihood divine,
its hours and ways of space,
its alphabet of time.

The great between is now
and time is ours to tell.
God comes and shows us how
to stand and walk and spell.
So life becomes a feast,
a round to set us free,
for God is first and last
and in between are we!

© 1975 Hope Publishing Company for USA and Canada and Stainer & Bell Ltd
for other territories

Whenever I am asked which of my own texts is my personal favourite, I shall always quote 'A hymn of first, last and in-between'. I wrote it in 1974 after I had helped to produce a radio programme in Geneva in honour of Duke Ellington who died early that year. The broadcast included an extract from one of Ellington's Sacred Concerts; the particular piece in question being the song 'In the beginning: God', with which he also starts his autobiography *Music is my mistress*. Doreen Potter wrote a tune for it which she dedicated to my wife, and which she called KANELLI (my wife's name being Elly). Of all the tunes Doreen Potter has composed for my texts, I judge this without a doubt to be her finest. This appears in *Break Not the Circle*.

57 I throw my rejoicing like birds to the heavens

12.12.12.12.8.

I throw my rejoicing like birds to the heavens.
Their tunes touch the treetops, the slumber awakening
of songs that are locked in the rocks and in crystals,
still sounding through death. And their fragments are breaking
to suns that are merged into God.

My ground for rejoicing is Christ in my inmost.
Creator of worlds, he was born in a stable;
he showed us God's love as from earth he was lifted.
From darkness he leads us to sit at his table
and none is forgotten by God.

My joy and rejoicing are found in the Spirit,
the generous fountain, and tongue beyond speaking.
God's people are one among people and races;
the chalice of blessing and pain we are taking,
we're drinking together in God.

Another Frostenson text translated from Swedish, but its origin is in Africa, in Ghana. The opening line, 'I throw my rejoicing like birds to the heavens' is taken from a Ghanaian prayer recorded by Fritz Pawelzik who was a youth leader with the Ghana YMCA and who published a collection of these prayers in a German translation in 1968. Frostenson wrote his text, based on the prayer mentioned, in 1969 and Torgny Erseus composed a tune REJOICINGS for it one year later, which can be found with this text in *Songs and Hymns from Sweden*.

58 'It's Jesus we want,' requested the Greeks

10 10.10.10 10.

'It's Jesus we want,' requested the Greeks.
And so, Lord, today, it's you whom we seek.
We know you are near, before and behind;
by you, only you, creation is signed;
by you, only you, creation is signed.

Sometimes in the streets of hurry and haste,
we happen to catch the light of your face;
a cry and a shout from deepest despair.
We stop and we know: it's you whom we hear;
we stop and we know: it's you whom we hear.

We know that you live in jungle and wood
with those who are bent on freedom's pursuit.
You take to the hills, their brother and friend,
till earth is again a home for mankind;
till earth is again a home for mankind.

Rejected by people, nailed to a cross,
you die but you rise, forever with us.
You, light of the age and formative word,
let freedom spring up and blossom on earth!
Let freedom spring up and blossom on earth!

Interesting one, this one! I was asked to translate Anders Frostenson's text, 'Vi ville dej se, så grekerna bad', for the 1973 edition of *Cantate Domino*. During the process of translation, it struck me that the ideas contained in the hymn sounded rather familiar, and upon enquiry, Dr. Frostenson admitted that his text was a paraphrase of one of my own texts: 'We meet you O Christ, in many a guise'! So here I was translating my own material back into English. While unhappy about the matter, I allowed myself to be persuaded to have the hymn included in *Cantate Domino*, as the editors were keen to retain the melody SEEKERS which Lars Åke Lundberg had composed for it in 1968. It is also found in *Songs and Hymns from Sweden* to the Lundberg tune.

59 A hymn for Good Shepherd Sunday

7.6.7.6.7 7.

Jesus, shepherd of our souls,
selfless in your caring,
lead us out to days of peace
and of thoughtful sharing.
Free our life from ill and war;
what is good in us restore.

Jesus, be our shepherd still,
though the settings alter;
grant us for our changing days
faith that will not falter.
Bless us in our modern scene
of computer and machine.

Living Lord, renew the charge
at your rising given:
that the church in love should bring
to this earth your heaven.
Give us insight, show us how
life is here, the task is now.

May we with a shepherd's heart
love the people round us,
still recalling how your love
in our straying found us.
Keep us, Lord, in humble ways,
lead us clearly all our days.

I wrote this especially for a BBC radio broadcast service in 1965 when Good Shepherd Sunday (second Sunday after Easter) fell on 2nd May, one day after May Day. As with my version of Psalm 23, I have tried to bring the idea of pastoral caring into the context of a modern technological world. We chose Erik Routley's tune VARNDEAN for it. In the 1972 edition of *Pilgrim Praise* the text is linked with SONG 13 by Orlando Gibbons (1583 - 1625).

60 A hymn on sharing bread and cup

11 11.11.5.

Let all who share one bread and cup remember
the oneness of that host of countless number
of those who are, as children of one Father,
part of each other.

If only we would live as sisters, brothers,
put faith to practice, truly care for others,
then we would do the will of him who sends us,
whose love attends us.

Use for yourself our highest and profoundest,
so that, O Lord, with everyone around us,
we may enjoy a world in Christ united,
so long awaited.

I was commissioned to translate a German hymn based on a J.A.Cramer text (1723 - 88) – 'Das sollt Ihr, Jesu Jünger, nie vergessen' – into English for *Cantate Domino*, where it is given with a melody LOBET DEN HERRN UND DANKT IHM, composed by Johann Crüger (1598 - 1662).

61 Till everyone is well and living

10 10.9.

Let Christian people practise praise and love
and let the clearness of their action prove
that Jesus Christ is well and living.

Let love be shared and passed like bread and wine,
and heart to heart be gen'rously inclined,
for Jesus Christ is well and living.

Let hope take shape in service and concern,
resourceful minds with human passion burn,
till everyone is well and living!

Written for the 1972 full music edition of *Pilgrim Praise* where it appears to Percy Buck's (1871 - 1947) delightful tune MARTINS.

62 Life itself an act of praise

8 9 8.8.

Let us our hearts and voices raise,
join to sing and live our grateful praise:
Lord, in your truth we put our trust;
your grace is great, your ways are just.

You broke the bondage of our past:
your concern for human life is vast.
Fulfil your work in us begun,
give us the mind of Christ the Son.

Lord, stir and charge your church anew,
so that Christians may be one in you.
Raise up your truth in every land
and help your people firm to stand.

Teach us, O Father, how to care,
and your love with all the world to share;
so be the sequence of our days,
and life itself, an act of praise!

When in 1969 a male voice choir of the Church of the Brethren in
Czechoslovakia came over to England for a concert tour, its conductor,
Dr. Bohumil Kejr, asked me to translate a few texts into English, among
them this one, which is reputed to be the oldest hymn coming out of
the Reformed tradition. Its author is Matej Kunvaldsky (1443 - 1500);
the tune dates from 1541. The original hymn consisted of 14 verses,
which in the process of translation were reduced to four.
In *Pilgrim Praise* it is associated with a traditional Czech tune now
named after the conductor as KEJR.

63 Communion calypso

8 8.10.10.10.8.
(including chorus)

Let us talents and tongues employ,
reaching out with a shout of joy:
bread is broken, the wine is poured,
Christ is spoken and seen and heard.
Jesus lives again, earth can breathe again,
pass the Word around: loaves abound!

Christ is able to make us one,
at the table he sets the tone,
teaching people to live to bless,
love in word and in deed express.
Chorus

Jesus calls us in, sends us out
bearing fruit in a world of doubt,
gives us love to tell, bread to share:
God (Immanuel) everywhere!
Chorus

Whereas normally a text is likely to exist before a tune is found or
written for it, in this case the process was reversed. Jamaican composer
Doreen Potter, who happened to be living in the same street as myself,
one day came and introduced an adapted Jamaican folksong known as
LINSTEAD. She asked me to write a text especially for it. I decided to
write a celebratory hymn for the eucharist: 'Communion calypso'. The
hymn was given its first international airing at the Nairobi Assembly of
the World Council of Churches in 1975 and was included in the
Worship Book for the 1983 Vancouver Assembly. This text can also
be found in *Break Not the Circle* and the *Hymnal Supplement*.

64 A hymn on doing God's word

8.7.8.7.
(Iambic)

Life could be good and rich and whole,
for God has well provided;
but we are from his will and aim
by greed and war divided.

They are God's children whom we kill,
with guns and resolutions,
and softly cradled is our will
in holy institutions.

They are his image, far and near,
in search of gracious neighbours,
who are equipped to lift and share
their daily fears and labours.

Happy are they who hear God's Word
and then go out to do it;
happy are they whose life and work
are given direction through it.

Lord, send us out, pursuing peace
with sisters and with brothers;
allow us still the earth to bless
through Christ, the Man for others.

Written for the Pilgrim Church in Plymouth in 1966 to J. S. Bach's tune
ACH GOTT UND HERR to which it appears in *Pilgrim Praise*. Professor
I-to Loh, then of Tainan Theological College, Taiwan, set it to one of
his own tunes and included the hymn in *New Songs of Asian Cities*.

65 From worship to service

11.11.11.5.

Lord, as we rise to leave this shell of worship,
called to the risk of unprotected living,
willing to be at one with all your people,
we ask for courage.

For all the strain with living interwoven,
for the demands each day will make upon us,
and for the love we owe the modern city,
Lord, make us cheerful.

Give us an eye for openings to serve you;
make us alert when calm is interrupted,
ready and wise to use the unexpected:
sharpen our insight.

Lift from our life the blanket of convention;
give us the nerve to lose our life to others.
Be with your church in death and resurrection,
Lord of all ages!

A major concern in my ministry has always been the making of a good
transition from worship to service, from celebration to action. This
hymn, written for the Pilgrim Church, is on that very theme.
Erik Routley wrote a new tune for it, WANSBECK, to which it is
printed in *Songs for the Seventies*. I introduced the hymn publicly at
a 'Come and Sing' event at Westminster Abbey in 1973. In that same
year, American composer, Ron Klusmeier wrote a new tune for the
hymn which he then included on a Vintage Record (SCV 132 Canada).
A tune LAMBHAY HILL by Philip Humphreys was included in
Pilgrim Praise.

66 A hymn of contrition

7 7.7 6.

Lord, confronted with your might,
with your purity and light
we are made with shame to see
all that we fail to be.

Conscious of our feeble will,
wanting good, but choosing ill,
we are sorry for our sin:
Lord, make us clean within.

Steady, Lord, our stumbling feet,
free our spirits from deceit.
Give us openness for pride;
we have no place to hide.

Lift us from despair and grief,
help us in our unbelief.
As we spread our hands to you,
fill us with life anew.

For the sake of Christ, forgive,
speak the Word, and we shall live.
Send us forward on our way,
Lord, with our heads held high.

'A hymn of contrition' written for *Break Not the Circle*. Doreen Potter wrote a tune for it which she called DUNN'S RIVER. Ron Klusmeier (USA) wrote a new melody for it, and the hymn is included on the double LP *Ron and Kris and Fred and Walter* (Kari Records, Canada, KRK 10375).

67 Kyrie

8 8 8.

Lord, do not hold yourself apart,
O Jesus-man, take us to heart
and set us free from guilt and smart.

Lord, search our hearts and know us well
and let the goodness of your spell
teach us to say: Immanuel!

Lord Jesus, hear our kyrie,
our sins forgive, our fears allay,
and let us see another day.

The second line of verse 2 uses the meaning 'gospel' = good spell. This text — a Kyrie — goes together with a metric Gloria No.**34**, both written for the 1972 edition of *Pilgrim Praise*. Christopher Bowers-Broadbent was commissioned by Stainer & Bell Ltd to compose a tune HAVERSTOCK.

68 A hymn for Rogation Day

6.6.6.6.

Lord God, we seek your face,
on you we must rely;
your never-measured grace
is ever standing by.

Give us your bread to eat,
sustain and make us whole
and with your wine complete
our joy of mind and soul.

To deep compassion move
the hearts of young and old;
grant on the seed of love
a harvest hundredfold. *

New visions bring to birth,
compel us to be one;
stir up your church on earth
for people to be won.

According to your will,
in Jesus' name we pray:
our deepest need fulfil,
our need of you today.

* cf. Luke 8: 8

© 1968 Hope Publishing Company for USA and Canada and Stainer & Bell Ltd
for other territories

Written for Rogation Sunday, the fifth after Easter, in 1965, for a
united act of worship in the St. Levan Valley Group of Churches,
Plymouth, of which the Pilgrim Church was an enthusiastic member.
We sang it to the tune ST. CECILIA (Leighton George Hayne,
1836 - 83), which is in *Pilgrim Praise*, together with a new melody NEW
VISIONS by H. W. Holmsen.

69 A hymn for growing Christians 11.10.11.10.

Lord God, who on the Friday of creation
conferred on us the freedom of the earth,
help us to make the most of all the choices
you set before us at the dawn of birth.

Give to your people confidence in striving
for life that is in faith and act complete;
redeem us from the blasphemy of praying
with lazy hands and unintending feet.

We want to BE! — so draw our will to Jesus
whose cross is planted on the day we're born;
then, help us to accept a life of Fridays,
to call them good, and live on love alone.

Lord, give us grace to honour you by choosing
the risk of growing up and taking care;
teach us, while wholly on your strength depending,
to live our life *as if* you were not there. *

* *so to speak!*

© 1985 Hope Publishing Company for USA and Canada and Stainer & Bell Ltd
for other territories

I wrote this text during the 1983 annual residential conference of the
moderators of the United Reformed Church. It arose out of a general
discussion in the meeting; we sang it in the closing communion service.
In the Genesis 'week' God made man/woman on the day before the
Sabbath. In Holy Week the crucifixion also fell on a Friday. So, living
a life of Fridays contains a double challenge - to celebrate each day as
'the first day of the rest of our life'; and daily to remember Christ's
self-sacrifice. The last two lines have already caused some consternation
among those of my friends who failed to spot the footnote! When we
first sang it, we used INTERCESSOR by C. H. H. Parry (1848 - 1918).

70 Psalm 8

8.7.8.7.
(Iambic)

Lord, how majestic is your name;
the earth and sky adore you,
the mouth of babies sings your praise
and children dance before you.

When I look up and see the stars
and think of space unending,
I marvel that you come and care,
us with your love befriending.

You lift us to the very height
of your creative likeness,
(just as you raised your Son from death
to Easter's wideawakeness).

This is one of several attempts to write metric versions of some of the Psalms. (*cf.* **52, 53, 87** and **89**). This version of Psalm 8 was incorporated in *Cantate Domino* to a tune specially composed for it by Margot Toplis who was from 1970 until 1972 secretary to the *Cantate Domino* editorial committee. In the 1972 edition of *Pilgrim Praise* this text appears to STORRINGTON by Eric Thiman (1900 - 1974).

71 A hymn for a funeral service

Lord of the living, in your name assembled,
we join to thank you for the life remembered.
Father, have mercy, to your children giving
  hope in believing.

Help us to treasure all that will remind us
of the enrichment in the days behind us.
Your love has set us in the generations,
  God of creation.

May we, whenever tempted to dejection,
strongly recapture thoughts of resurrection.
You gave us Jesus to defeat our sadness
  with Easter gladness.

Lord, you can lift us from the grave of sorrow
into the presence of your own tomorrow;
give to your people for the day's affliction
  your benediction.

© 1968 Hope Publishing Company for USA and Canada and Stainer & Bell Ltd
for other territories

Among the many frustrations of having to live with the traditional
hard-cover hymnbook in my pastoral ministry (and *Congregational
Praise* was an excellent book by any standards) was the absence of good
funeral hymns. So I added one to my early collection of *Pilgrim Praise*
which we, at the Pilgrim Church, Plymouth, used as a modest
supplement to Congregational Praise. Stanley L. Osborne, secretary of
the Hymn Book committee of the Anglican and United Churches of
Canada, has said of this text that 'its strength consists in its objective
character and its emphasis upon Easter'. In the first edition of *Pilgrim
Praise* we linked it with DIVA SERVATRIX (Bayeux Church Melody
ascribed to Pierre Daniel Huet, 1630 - 1721), while in the full melody
edition of 1972 it appears to CHRISTE SANCTORUM, first published
in 1782.

72 Freedom and unity add up

6.5.6.5.
and chorus 5.5.5.4.

Love has come among us!
Christ is on our side,
leads us into freedom;
life is high and wide.
Free and one make life,
love is bread and cup;
one and free make sense:
(clap hands)
it all adds up.

Jesus, emptied, broken,
makes his people whole,
fills us with his fullness,
helps us fill our role.
Chorus

Christ, triumphant, living,
makes us fall in love
with his world of people,
world of share-believe.
Chorus

Jesus goes before us
on the road of faith,
with his theo-logic
staying close to life.
Chorus

God-and-man among us,
Christ is all in all:
love incarnate figures,
freedom rings a bell!
Chorus

I hate to admit it, but I wrote this song during a major address at the 1975 Nairobi Assembly of the World Council of Churches. The presentation was long and wordy and we had the printed text in front of us anyway . . . . . So I switched off and 'did my own thing'. The refrain of the song was inspired by the Assembly theme, 'Jesus Christ frees and unites':

> Free and one make life,
> love is bread and cup;
> One and free make sense:
> it all adds up

A Russian interpreter asked me during the Assembly (with a twinkle in his eye), if I did not know that 'three and one make four'? God's arithmetic is higher than ours! Doreen Potter, who - like myself - was an adviser on worship in Nairobi, wrote a tune NAIROBI for it there and then; Peter Janssens, the German composer and pop group leader arranged it, and we sang it several times during the Assembly, including it also in the closing act of worship. The song appears on the LP *Break down the walls* (Pietbiet Records 1024).

73 Made to walk the road of need

12 12.12.

By each other sentenced to walk the road of need,
people are divided in camps of caste and creed.
Jesus is Lord for the welfare of the people.

People are divided in camps of rich and poor.
Guests at wealthy parties have beggars at their door.
Jesus is Lord for the welfare of the people.

People die of hunger; they die of want and shame.
Others in their comfort don't want to know their name.
Jesus is Lord for the welfare of the people.

Children are abandoned in modern city streets,
gutters for a mattress and newsprint for their sheets.
Jesus is Lord for the welfare of the people.

All the tears of millions become a sea of pain,
by the shame of hunger the street of life is stained.
Jesus is Lord for the welfare of the people.

Welfare of the nations and liberating word,
God's great gift to people is Jesus, Man and Lord.
Jesus is Lord for the welfare of the people.

Originally, the first line of this hymn ran: 'Men condemn each other to walk the road of need'. This text is a paraphrase of a Marathi text by Devdatta B. Kamble, and is included in the 1972 collection *New Songs of Asian Cities*. Early that year I had been invited to Jakarta, Indonesia, to act as a text consultant to the editor of a book which was to contain 'explicit expressions of Christian faith in the urban context of Asia'. Initiative for the project had been taken by the Christian Conference of Asia's Urban and Industrial Mission Committee. In practice, my involvement during the ten-day meetings consisted of putting into English verse various texts from Asia which the editor, Professor I-to Loh of Taiwan had collected and recorded among Asian city people. It turned out to be one of the most exhilarating and demanding experiences I have ever had in the field of hymn-writing and translation. The tune, which is Indian, is entitled ABHANG.

74 Nesta grande cidade

10.10.12.10.

Modern people have cities for their home,
where their life is walled in by want and dread,
pained by nights without sleep and days of grinding work,
in the struggle to earn their daily bread.

In our cities, immense and growing out,
there are millions from faith and love estranged,
who need to recapture thoughts of better things
and whose hearts, by the grace of Christ, can change.

In the dark of our noisy city life,
men and women are groping for the light,
human beings who hunger to see right prevail,
unaware of the liberating Christ.

In the great giant cities of our globe,
hollowed out by the ways of greed and crime,
we are set to reflect the likeness of our God
and to act out renewal's great design.

Grow then, cities, to house the human race,
with your skyscrapers blotting out the sun.
Let Christ be the light to shine from all our homes
in the high-rising blocks of steel and stone.

A translation from Portuguese, commissioned for *Cantate Domino*. The original text, 'Nesta grande cidade vivemos', is by Professor João Dias de Araujo (b. 1930), Reformed theologian and poet in Brazil. The music is also by a Brazilian, the well-known organist João W. Faustini, (b. 1931).

75 Move me to crying, silence and earth

Move me to crying, silence and earth
and to the table, breaking the bread.

Broken your true love, open your wound,
crying through torment till we are found.

You are the author — come, live in me;
living for others, I shall be free.

This contemplative text is a translation from Anders Frostenson's Swedish original, written in 1966. The tune SILENCE AND EARTH composed for it is by Stig Gustav Schonberg. The hymn is included in *Songs and Hymns from Sweden.*

76 My longing is older than light years of sun

11.11.11.11.
(Anapaestic)

My longing is older than light years of sun.
Today I will come as a guest in your home.
A prophet, Zacchaeus, you came out to see?
I saw you from far, long before you saw me.

You dropped for a moment your rank and repute
and you are a child in the presence of God.
You hid with the rich in the ghetto of wealth;
let go of your fear and abandon your stealth!

The money you have is no more than a loan.
The money is God's, you are Abraham's son.
Be merry, Zacchaeus, come out through the gate,
for you and your house are to live in the light.

Another Frostenson text, based on *Luke 19: 1-10*: 'Min längtan är äldre än solarnas ljus', written in 1969. The melody LIVE IN THE LIGHT for it was composed by Karl-Olof Robertson in 1974. The original, like so many other Swedish hymns that appear in the anthology, *Songs and Hymns from Sweden* in English translation, is included in the experimental supplement *Psalmer och Visor* to the Swedish Lutheran Hymnbook.

77 A hymn for baptism (1)

Now in the name of him, who sent
to preach by word and sacrament,
upon this new-born child we pray
the strength of God in doubtful day.

Our names are written in his hand;
he leads us to the promised land.
We rise in wonder from the flood
and love becomes our livelihood.

With Noah, through disaster borne,
with Moses, from the river drawn
with Jonah, from the sea released,
we celebrate this rising feast.

The water is a seal and sign
of costly love that makes us clean.
This love we see in Christ portrayed,
who rose triumphant from the dead.

We sing our thanks that old and young
so to the church of Christ belong.
This is the covenant of grace:
we look salvation in the face.

Among the several inadequacies of the traditional hymnbook with which I had to work, I found the absence of good baptismal and post-communion hymns particularly difficult. Consequently, my first texts were generally hymns on these themes. Water is a symbol of both birth and death. The hymn incorporates early Christian thoughts that link the sacrament of baptism with Old Testament traditions. This hymn was written in 1964 for the Pilgrim Church. We sang it to HERONGATE, an English traditional melody from Essex, as arranged in the *English Hymnal. Pilgrim Praise* gives in addition a newly commissioned tune THE SEAL OF LOVE by H. W. Holmsen.

78 A hymn for harvest thanksgiving

9.8.9.8.
(Anapaestic)

Now join we, to praise the creator,
our voices in worship and song;
we stand to recall with thanksgiving
that to him all seasons belong.

We thank you, O God, for your goodness,
for the joy and abundance of crops,
for food that is stored in our larders,
for all we can buy in the shops.

But also of need and starvation
we sing with concern and despair,
of skills that are used for destruction,
of land that is burnt and laid bare.

We cry for the plight of the hungry
while harvests are left on the field,
for orchards neglected and wasting,
for produce from markets withheld.

The song grows in depth and in wideness;
the earth and its people are one.
There can be no thanks without giving,
no words without deeds that are done.

Then teach us, O Lord of the harvest,
to be humble in all that we claim;
to share what we have with the nations,
to care for the world in your name.

Peter Cutts, chairman of the committee that published *New Church Praise* succinctly sums up this text: ' . . . a welcome recognition in a harvest hymn that abundance of crops is not universal'. It has become widely known since it appeared in the *New Catholic Hymnal* to an excellent tune HARVEST by Geoffrey Laycock, who is head of music at Keswick College of Education, Norwich. This is a perfect example of sensitively matching music and text. It was included in one of the 1973 'Come and Sing' sessions at Westminster Abbey. Ron Klusmeier gave it his own musical treatment on the successful LP *Thank you that now is the time of our life* (Vintage Records SCV 132, Canada). Introduction in the USA was made in *Ecumenical Praise*, where it appears to the tune SHARING by Austin Lovelace, the well-known Methodist composer and organist in Denver, Colorado.

79 A hymn for after the communion (2) L.M.

Now let us from this table rise
renewed in body, mind and soul;
with Christ we die and live again,
his selfless love has made us whole.

With minds alert, upheld by grace,
to spread the Word in speech and deed,
we follow in the steps of Christ,
at one with all in hope and need.

To fill each human house with love,
it is the sacrament of care;
the work that Christ began to do
we humbly pledge ourselves to share.

Then grant us courage, Father-God,
to choose again the pilgrim way,
and help us to accept with joy
the challenge of tomorrow's day.

Another hymn written for 'the gaps' (*cf.* **77**), and first used at the
Pilgrim Church, Plymouth in 1964. Originally sung to BOURTON (Eric
Thiman 1900 - 1974), the full music edition of *Pilgrim Praise* suggests
TALLIS' CANON, but the most widely used combination of text and
tune is now generally with the Swiss traditional melody SOLOTHURN
with which it appeared in *New Church Praise*. *Ecumenical Praise*
introduced it on the North American scene to DEUS TUORUM
MILITUM, a Grenoble church melody. The words 'the sacrament of
care' (verse 3, line 2) were used as the theme of the 14th International
Assembly of the World Federation of Diaconal Associations, held at
Warwick University, Great Britain, in July 1983, and the hymn itself
was adopted as the theme song of the assembly. Compare the
Authorised Version of *Acts 1: 1* to the line in verse 3, 'the work that
Christ began to do'.

80 A hymn on celebrating life
13.10.12.10.

Now let us translate in the language of human-ness
all we have heard with our ears and our tongue,
fully committed to beautiful holiness,
placed in a world where we gladly belong.

Appointed to spending a life of creativeness,
let us, with all who inhabit the globe,
worship the God who gives freedom for timidness,
feasting together on laughter and hope.

Let life be a song of devotion and cheerfulness,
let us say 'yes' to the goodness of God,
and in our love-making, friendships and tenderness
praise him who loves us in flesh and in blood.

This text was written for the 1972 full music edition of *Pilgrim Praise* to the tune WAS LEBET, WAS SCHWEBET (1754). Tom Harpur, religious editor of the *Toronto Star,* wrote on 26th January, 1974, that this hymn 'scores what is undoubtedly a first in the history of Christian hymnology by calling on the singers to praise God in their love-making'. So much for Nietzsche's 'pale Galilean'.

81 A marriage hymn

10 10.10 10.

O God from whom mankind derives its name,
whose covenant of grace remains the same,
be with these two who now before you wait;
enlarge the love they come to consecrate.

May through their union other lives be blessed;
their door be wide to stranger and to guest,
Give them the understanding that is kind,
grant them the blessing of an open mind.

Preserve their days from inwardness of heart:
to each the gift of truthfulness impart.
Their bond be strong against all strain and strife
amid the changes of this earthly life.

From stage to stage on life's unfolding way
bring to their mind the vows they make this day,
your spirit be their guide in every move;
their faith in Christ the basis of their love.

Lord, bless us all to whom this day brings joy,
let no events our unity destroy,
and help us, till all sense of time is lost,
to live in love and not to count the cost.

What I have said about the dearth of hymns on baptism and that critical moment of breaking bread at the altar and then applying it in sharing bread and Christ with the people of our world also applies to texts to celebrate a wedding. So here is my contribution to the worship life of the Pilgrim Church on the occasions of marriage services. The 1972 edition of *Pilgrim Praise* suggests two tunes: FFIGYSBREN (Welsh, 1840) and a newly commissioned tune BUNTY by Alan Ridout.

82 A hymn on Abrahamic faith

C.M.

O God of the eternal now,
why is your church so slow?
What is it that prevents us all
from growing up to go?

If, Lord, it is our love of ease
by which we thwart your plan,
then call us out, unsettle us
and lead us by the hand.

May we with courage take the risk
and leave the past behind
to be a people on the move,
throw caution to the wind.

Give us the heart of Abraham,
for changes make us bold;
and bless us only so that we
in turn may bless the world.

A hymn about Abrahamic faith, inspired by Bishop Lesslie Newbigin's story about the negotiations that eventually led to the formation of the Church of South India. He tells somewhere that, irritated by the people who asked for copper-bottomed guarantees at every point of the union conversations, the committee chairman told them that Christians are people who have no right to keep asking where they are going. Risk-taking is one of the major themes in the Bible. At the Pilgrim Church we sang it to ST. STEPHEN (William Jones, 1726 - 1800). Christopher Bowers-Broadbent wrote a new tune DORIS for it in 1972 for *Pilgrim Praise*. Kris Klusmeier sings it on the Vintage Records LP (SCV 132, 1973) to a melody composed by her husband Ron.

83 A hymn on the Holy Spirit 10 9.11 9.4.

O Holy Spirit, hear us as we pray:
renew your people's faith day by day.
Free us from the chaos of night and deepness;
in our life and death cheer and keep us.
    Kyrieleis.

Uproot and teach us by your restless love
the art of sharing all we are and have;
that with strong affection, in truth and doing,
we may love your law, peace pursuing.
    Kyrieleis.

You plead our cause, and by your gift of peace
our lives are from fear of death released.
How we need your presence, O gift from heaven,
all our words and deeds to enliven.
    Kyrieleis.

A paraphrase of Martin Luther's 'Nun bitten wir den heiligen Geist'. I wrote it for the 1970 Uniting Assembly of the International Congregational Council (of which I was general secretary at the time) and the World Alliance of Reformed Churches. We sang it to a pre-reformation tune VORREFORMATORISCH from the Johann Walther *Gesangbuch* (1524) at the uniting act of worship in St. Andrew's Church, Nairobi, on 20th August 1970. This tune appears in *Pilgrim Praise*.

84 Seigneur, rassemble nous

7.6.7.6.
and chorus 6.7.

Our faults divide and hinder;
your grace can make us one;
we wonder at your rising,
your light is like the sun.
*Unite us, Lord, in peace
and uphold us with your love.*

You are our expectation
in loneliness and pain;
your healing and your pardon
are greater than our sin.
Chorus

Lord, look upon the starving
and set the captive free,
Share out among the people
the bread of unity.
Chorus

How happy are the people
who strive to be at one,
who live as sisters, brothers,
who lay their hatred down.
Chorus

O Lord, whose silent spirit
enlightens and endows,
make us in faith receptive
and help us love your house.
Chorus

Your cross will draw together
the circle of mankind;
in you shall all the people
their true communion find.
Chorus

Death can no longer hurt us,
triumphant is your word.
Let life now grow and blossom,
O Jesus, risen Lord!
Chorus

The original French text of this hymn on unity and peace is by Dominique Ombrie (b. 1933) who also composed the tune. The translation was commissioned for the 1974 edition of *Cantate Domino*.

85 A hymn for Christmas

Our God has given his Son to the earth,
a Father's love has brought Christmas to birth.
Life now unfolds in the light of the day,
Jesus is present, the feast is to stay.

He holds the future, the present, the past;
the fact of Christmas was given to last.
Let us then see in the coming of Christ:
love is the gift and the church is the feast.

Of incarnation the church is the sign,
the given token of hope for mankind,
bringing us under the good of its spell:
God is among us, each day is noel.

A Christmas carol for the Pilgrim Church. In the third line of verse 3 note the 'good of its spell' (good spell = gospel). Its first line was inspired by the old Flemish carol 'Er is een kindeke geboren op d'aard', to be sung to an original FLEMISH CAROL in the *Oxford Book of Carols* as arranged by the Dutch composer Julius Röntgen. In the music edition of *Pilgrim Praise* it also appears to a tune HENRICUS by Christopher Bowers-Broadbent. Ron Klusmeier composed a melody for it which is included in the double LP album *Ron and Kris and Fred and Walter* (Kari Records, Canada, KRK 10375).

86 A hymn for baptism (2)

8.7.8.7.D.
including chorus

Out of deep, unordered water
God created land and life;
world of bird and beast, and later
two-some people, husband, wife.
There is water in the river
bringing life to tree and plant.
Let creation praise its giver:
there is water in the font.

Water on the human forehead,
birthmark of the love of God,
is the sign of death and rising;
through the seas there runs a road.
Chorus

Standing round the font reminds us
of the Hebrews' climb ashore.
Life is hallowed by the knowledge:
God has been this way before.
Chorus

A baptismal hymn, using a mixture of biblical imagery, written for the
Pilgrim Church in 1965. Compare the last line of verse 2 with *Exodus
14: 22* and the second line of verse 3 with *Corinthians 10: 1-2*.
Bernard Warren, our organist there, made a brilliant suggestion for its
musical treatment: We sang the verse to DRAKE'S BROUGHTON by
Edward Elgar (1857 - 1934), with the refrain to the English traditional
melody SHIPSTON. The music edition of *Pilgrim Praise* offers a new
tune THERE IS WATER by H. W. Holmsen.
  At the 1984 Spring Synod of the West Midlands Province of the
United Reformed Church, during a debate on 'Baptism, Eucharist and
Ministry', we sang it to AUSTRIA which was surprisingly effective.

87 Psalm 130

C.M.

Out of our failure to create
a world of love and care;
out of the depths of human life
we cry to God in prayer.

Out of the darkness of our time,
of days for ever gone,
our souls are longing for the light,
like watchmen for the dawn.

Out of the depths we cry to him
whose will is strong and just;
all human hole and corner ways
are by his light exposed.

Hope in the Lord whose timeless love
gives laughter where we wept;
the Father, who at every point
his word has given and kept.

© 1968 Hope Publishing Company for USA and Canada and Stainer & Bell Ltd
for other territories

This metrical paraphrase was written for the first edition of *Pilgrim Praise* in 1967. Verse 3 in the text draws on *John 3: 19-21*. Tunes suggested for it in the music edition of *Pilgrim Praise* are WALSALL from Anchor's *Psalmody*, 1721; and DEMPSEY specially composed for it by Alan Ridout in 1972. In *New Church Praise* it appears to OSBORNE by Henry Carey (1692? - 1743).

88 A psalm for today

6.4.6.4.10.10.

Out of our night of day,
darkness at noon,
we cry: Lord, come and make
your presence known.
Lord Jesus, come and help our shaky faith
and make us strong to face the pain of life.

Into our night of day
come with your light,
and let your Spirit heal
all hurt of fright.
Fulfil our hollow days that make no sense
and leave us not in life without defence.

Redeem our hearts for love,
free us from fear;
let crying in the night
make way for cheer.
Lord, help us keep the promise you have made;
bring in the day when none shall be afraid.

'A psalm for today', says the title. It was first included in *Break Not the Circle* to Doreen Potter's tune WYNONE. American theologian and composer, Carlton R. Young wrote an effectively moving tune for it, based on the motif of 'Aus tiefer Not schrei ich zu dir', from J. S. Bach's *Cantate No.38*. The text is, of course, not unrelated to the trend of thought that runs through Psalm 130. The hymn, to Young's melody DAYLIGHT, was published in *Choirbook for Saints and Singers*.

89 Psalm 150

7 7.7 7.

Praise the Lord with joyful cry;
let the mood of praise run high.
Praise him who with mighty deeds
human greatness far exceeds.

Praise him with the sound that swings,
with percussion, brass and strings.
Let the world at every chance
praise him with a song and dance.

Praise with life and voice the Lord,
him who speaks in deed and word,
who to life the world ordained:
let our praise be unrestrained!

A straightforward paraphrase of *Psalm 150* 'with percussion, brass and strings'. Written for the Pilgrim Church to NORTHAMPTON (Charles John King, 1859 - 1934), it later became very popular in conjunction with a tune specially composed for it by the Australian clergyman and composer Canon Lawrence Francis Bartlett (b. 1933) who, in fact, called the tune ONE-FIFTY. *Pilgrim Praise* suggests MONKLAND (J. A. Freylinghausen, 1670 - 1739; arranged by J. B. Wilkes, 1785 - 1869). *Ecumenical Praise* opts for Bartlett's tune, and gives in addition a marvellous descant by John Wilson, formerly Director of Music of Charterhouse and on the staff of the Royal College of Music, and one of the enthusiastic leaders of the Hymn Society of Great Britain and Ireland.

90 A May Day offering hymn

11 11.11.7.
and chorus 14 13.

Raising our hands as a sign of rejoicing,
and with our lips our togetherness voicing,
giving ourselves to a life of creativeness,
worship and work must be one!
Worship the Lord, worship the Father, the Spirit, the Son
raising our hands in devotion to him who is one.

Praying and training that we be a blessing
and by our workmanship daily expressing
we are committed to serving humanity,
worship and work must be one!
Chorus

Called to be partners with God in creation,
honouring Christ as the Lord of the nation,
we must be ready for risk and for sacrifice,
worship and work must be one!
Chorus

Bringing the bread and the wine to the table,
asking that we may be led and enabled,
truly united, to build new communities,
worship and work must be one!
Chorus

Now in response to the life you are giving,
help us, O Father, to offer our living,
seeking a just and a healing society,
worship and work must be one!
Chorus

Based on a May Day offering hymn from Sri Lanka this hymn became popular through its inclusion in *Cantate Domino* to a traditional Sri Lankan melody and its being used widely at the 1975 Nairobi Assembly of the World Council of Churches. A new tune specially composed for it by Ron Klusmeier, and hand-movements devised for it by Kris Klusmeier, have given this hymn a new lease of life and wide popularity in Canada and the USA. The words of the refrain, 'Worship the Lord' have become the title of a substantial collection of Klusmeier material. The song also features on an LP *Song circling all the earth* (Praise Records PRS 369).

91 See how swarming birds of heaven 8.7.8.7.

See how swarming birds of heaven
fly into the Lord's embrace;
how for plant and vine and forest
God provides a fruitful place.

See how people, tight and selfish,
cling to life and search for gain,
driven by their want of winning,
turning like a weather-vane.

See how Christ in utter freedom
gives away his life for all,
sharing what the Father gives him:
life the present, love the call.

Jesus shows us how the Father
wills that human life should be:
Free as birds that wing to heaven,
strong and rising, like a tree.

A translation from Swedish of a 1971 Göran Bexell text 'Se på himlens många fåglar', to a tune BIRDS OF HEAVEN of the same year by Lasse Angeborn, which is in *Songs and Hymns from Sweden*. For verse 2 *cf. Ecclesiastes 1: 14.*

92 Seek your rest

12.5.12.5.

Seek your rest in the storm winds that cover the moors,
seek refuge in God;
in the light of the sea and the grass underfoot,
seek refuge in God.

Seek your rest among people where living is strain,
seek refuge in God;
in the tears that dissolve the fatigue and the pain,
seek refuge in God.

Seek your rest in the Word, put your trust in the Son,
seek refuge in God;
in the love that is pure and can cleanse us from sin,
seek refuge in God.

A translation from the Swedish of a 1969 Anders Frostenson text, for the 1976 collection *Songs and Hymns from Sweden*. The melody SEEK YOUR REST is from Göte Stransjö.

93 Magnificat Now!

L.M.

Sing we a song of high revolt;
make great the Lord, his name exalt!
Sing we the song that Mary sang
of God at war with human wrong.

Sing we of him who deeply cares
and still with us our burden bears.
He who with strength the proud disowns,
brings down the mighty from their thrones.

By him the poor are lifted up;
he satisfies with bread and cup
the hungry ones of many lands;
the rich must go with empty hands.

He calls us to revolt and fight
with him for what is just and right,
to sing and live Magnificat
in crowded street and council flat.

cf. Luke 1: 46-55

This text, Magnificat Now!, became the centre of quite a controversy in the House of Commons in 1972. The hymn, which is a fairly straightforward contemporary version of the Song of Mary, was incorporated in a school hymnal *New Life*. To quote a line from the satirical weekly *Punch*, 19th April 1972: 'The outcry over the left-wing hymnbook 'New Life', of which 50,000 copies have been sold to English schools, has led to hundreds of parents writing to (then Conservative M.P.) Enoch Powell'. Questions were put in Parliament; BBC-tv devoted a major programme to it and *Punch* gave us a whole page with 'samples from the other extreme'. Some West German churchleaders were also unsettled by the German translation of this text, and complained in *Lutherische Monatshefte* (January 1975). The fact that Stainer & Bell, in the 1972 edition of *Pilgrim Praise*, set it to the carol tune TANNENBAUM, better known as that of the Red Flag did not help either, although the whole controversy did marvels for the sale of *New Life*! The addition of the exclamation mark in the title came later. It goes back to the day when my friend and WCC colleague, Harry Daniel, a priest of the Church of South India, was released from a Manila prison after detention for his involvement in urban industrial mission activities in the Philippines capital. The first words he spoke to me when we met after his release were: 'Magnificat Now!' Ever since then, there has been an exclamation mark in the title. In parts of South East Asia, some people have even coined the phrase: 'Magnificat Now' theology. The text was originally written for local worship at the Pilgrim Church, Plymouth, in Advent 1965. Other tunes to which this text can be sung include TUGWOOD by Nicholas Gatty in *Pilgrim Praise* or Doreen Potter's ST. MARY'S in *Cantate Domino*.

94 People matter

8.7.8.7.D.

Sing we of the modern city,
scene alike of joy and stress;
sing we of its nameless people
in their urban wilderness.
Into endless rows of houses
life is set a million-fold,
life expressed in human beings
daily born and growing old.

In the city full of people,
world of speed and hectic days;
in the ever changing setting
of the latest trend and craze,
Christ is present, and among us,
in the crowd, we see him stand.
In the bustle of the city
Jesus Christ is Everyman.

God is not remote in heaven
but on earth to share our shame;
changing graph and mass and numbers
into persons with a name.
Christ has shown, beyond statistics,
human life with glory crowned;
by his timeless presence proving:
people matter, people count!

This text was unashamedly sparked off by my negative reaction to the hymn 'Sing we of the golden city, pictured in the legends old . . .' by Felix Adler (1851 - 1933). Having lived in cities most of my life, and having visited some of the most 'soul-less' capitals of this world, it has always struck me how desperately necessary it is to sing of the modern, rather than of the golden city, and to stress the basic message of the Gospel, that people matter, especially in the concrete anonymity and deprivation that are such typical symptoms of the urbanisation of our time. Doreen Potter wrote a melody TAVERNAY for it, about which she has said: 'I was struck by words like stress, speed, hectic, ever-changing, bustle, all invoking a tension. The melody came into my mind as I read the text, but the problem was whether to write it down as 5/4; 6/4 and 4/4 in alternate bars; or in its present form. In any case, the tension between melody and accompaniment should be obvious'. This is in *Pilgrim Praise* and *Cantate Domino*.

American composer Ronald Arnatt, wrote a tune for it, especially for the Episcopal Supplement *More Hymns and Spiritual Songs*.

95 A workers' hymn

10 13. 7 6. 9.

Son of the Father, Jesus, Lord and slave,
born among the cattle in the squalor of a cave,
one with God, you made yourself
one with us, shunning wealth;
Lord, we worship you with hand and mind.

Son of the Father, Jesus, workers' friend,
you whom Joseph taught the skills of working with your hand,
man, at home in builder's yard,
one with us, toiling hard;
Lord, we worship you with hand and mind.

Son of the Father, author of our faith,
choosing men to follow you from every walk of life,
who with them, in boats, on shore,
troubles shared, burdens bore;
Lord, we worship you with hand and mind.

Seed of the Father, from life's furrow born,
teaching men in parables from agriculture drawn,
Jesus, lover of the soil,
Man of earth, son of toil;
Lord, we worship you with hand and mind.

Father and Spirit, Jesus, Lord and Man,
bless us in the work you have appointed to be done.
Lift our spirits, guide our wills,
steer our hands, use our skills;
Lord, we worship you with hand and mind.

I translated this text under great pressure from a Sri Lankan original for
the hymnbook *New Songs of Asian Cities*, in which it appears under the
title 'The Workers' Hymn' to a traditional Sri Lankan melody, now
named WORKER, and suggested for a May Day service.

96 A hymn of creative love

Surrounded by a world of need,
by cries for healing, housing, bread,
our mind is given to despair,
and hope is undermined by war.

Yet through the fabric of our time
there runs the liberating theme
of love that makes the world go round,
of love creative and profound.

This love is in the face of Christ,
in human life, made manifest;
its strong intent will conquer all,
it raises people when they fall.

Then help us, Lord, to understand
the claims and blessings of your plan,
and use, to bring your reign about,
those in the church and those without.

Written in 1966 for the Pilgrim Church, Plymouth, to FULDA
(Gardiner's *Sacred Melodies*, 1812). It was included in the United
Reformed Church's *New Church Praise* to a melody ASKERSWELL
specially composed for it by Peter Cutts (b. 1937). In *Pilgrim Praise*,
Orlando Gibbons's ANGEL'S SONG or a melody PELOQUIN by
C. A. Peloquin, is suggested.

97 The present tense

10 10.10 10.
(Dactyllic)

Thank you, O Lord, for the time that is now,
for all the newness your minutes allow;
make us alert with your presence of mind,
keep us alive to the claims of mankind.

Thank you, O Lord, for the time that is past,
for all the values and thoughts that will last.
May we all stagnant tradition ignore,
leaving behind things that matter no more.

Thank you for hopes of the day that will come,
for all the change that will happen in time;
Lord, for the future our spirits prepare,
hallow our doubts and redeem us from fear.

Make us afraid of the thoughts that delay,
faithful in all the affairs of to-day;
keep us, our father, from playing it safe,
thank you that now is the time of our life!

This is another of those hymns which have found wide favour with hymnbook committees around the world. The text is an attempt at spelling out our priorities as far as our use and evaluation of time are concerned. I wrote it for the Pilgrim Church with the tune QUEDLINBURGH in mind (Johann Christian Kittel, the 18th century German composer). This is in *Pilgrim Praise* with DURLEY, a setting by Peter Tranchell. Ron Klusmeier gave it his own musical treatment, very effectively, on an LP named after this hymn, *Thank you that now is the time of our life* (Vintage Records, Canada, SCV 132). For those singers who want to do a bit of thinking: the use of the word *minutes* in verse 1 is deliberately meant to be two-fold, (i) minutes as units of time; and (ii) minutes as a record of things that have happened. Think of 'predestination', foreknowledge, 'perfectum propheticum'.

112

98 A hymn on right stewardship

7.6.7.6.D.

The earth, the sky, the oceans
and all that they contain,
the world with all its secrets,
they are the Lord's domain.
To rule his great creation,
God shares with humankind
his gifts of strength and courage
and an inventive mind.

To us from birth is given
our stewardship and brief:
to search for truth and purpose,
to find the heart of life.
God calls us to adventure
with work of hand and brain;
to share with all his people
the profits we may gain.

For quest and exploration,
our God has given the key
to free the hidden forces
and wealth of soil and sea.
To new advance in science,
research to conquer pain,
to growth in skill and knowledge
we are by God ordained.

We pledge ourselves to service,
that with the help of Christ
we may be able stewards
of all things that exist.
Whatever we discover,
on earth or out in space,
God grant that we may use it
to bless the human race.

Written for the celebration of the 100th anniversary of the birth of Robert Falcon Scott, the Antarctic explorer (1868 - 1912), who was born and who grew up in the Milehouse area of Plymouth. The anniversary was marked by a civic service at St. Bartholomew's Church of England, and the hymn was commissioned for the occasion by the priest-in-charge, the Rev. John Herklots. The hymn was sung to PEARSALL (Robert Lucas de Pearsall, 1795 - 1856). In *Pilgrim Praise* this text is set to SWANMORE by Peter Tranchell.

99 On familiar ground

10 10. 10 10.

The fullness of the earth is God's alone
and life's unfolding is divinely known.
With humble hearts we recognize the claim
that every child and nation bears his name.

Not only his a world of field and flower;
to him belongs the scene of stack and tower.
His love is focussed on the city street,
and on canteens where busy people meet.

On wards and sites, in workshops and in schools,
in work of mind and skilfulness with tools,
we feel his presence in our daily round:
the place on which we stand is holy ground.

Then let us every given morning pray
that we may sanctify the city's day;
that Christ may guard our going out and in
and choose through us the world in love to win.

My preoccupation with the challenges of Christian discipleship in a
contemporary, urbanised and industrialised world prompted me to
write this text for the Pilgrim Church, Plymouth, in 1967, and it was
sparked off by a sermon I preached on the calling of Moses, in
Exodus 3 'the place where you are standing is holy ground' (NEB). We
sang it to CHILTON FOLIAT (George Clement Martin, 1844 - 1916),
but the full music edition of *Pilgrim Praise* suggests FARLEY CASTLE
(Henry Lawes, 1596 - 1662) as well as a new melody MORESTEAD
specially composed for this text by Peter Tranchell.

100 Hymn of the ten words

8.8.8.8.
and chorus 8 8.

The great commandment of our Lord:
translating language into deed
and giving shape to spoken word,
creating life from clay of creed.
Praise God, whose word and deed are one,
creative Spirit, human Son!

Ten times, for every finger once,
he spoke and all things came to be,
Ten times the Lord of life pronounced
the words that set his people free.
Praise God, whose word and deed are one,
creative Spirit, human Son!

The hands of God create and guide;
he goes before us on our way.
He gives his Word to take our side
and hallow each surprising day.
Praise God, whose word and deed are one,
creative Spirit, human Son!

Lord, use our hands to care and bless,
and make us fluent in your speech.
Help us to be what we profess,
to re-present your love to each.
Bring through us all the day to birth
when word and deed are one on earth.

Entitled 'Hymn of the ten words', this text was written for *Break Not the Circle*, and was inspired by the fascinating discovery that in the story of the creation, in *Genesis 1* it is written ten times that 'God said . . . ' and the realisation that what we call the Ten Commandments in *Exodus 20* are called the Ten Words by the Jews (*cf.* also Deca-logue!) (see v.2). The creation of the world and the way in which the people of God live in it are inextricably bound up. For the rest, the hymn expresses my strong preoccupation with the need to 'translate language into deed, give shape to the spoken word, and create life from clay of creed'. Doreen Potter wrote a tune for it, CAENWOOD. The hymn is also included, among others, on the LP *Ron and Kris and Fred and Walter* (Kari Records, Canada, KRK 10375) to a tune by Ron Klusmeier.

101 A back-to-front hymn (for the young in heart)

The language of the Hebrews
is right-to-left in print;
the end is the beginning,
their books are back to front.

The end is the beginning:
at Easter it began;
our life is topsy turvy,
for Jesus lives again.

Our life is topsy turvy,
the world is upside down.
The news that Christ is risen
has made us go to town.

The news that Christ is risen
has made the people's day!
We turn our hand to living;
the stone is rolled away.

I wrote this text for a family service on Easter-day 1968, at the Pilgrim Church, Plymouth, when we sang it to ST. ALPHEGE (Henry John Gauntlett, 1805 - 76). The title of the hymn describes its object. It tries to convey what the Germans call 'die Umwertung aller Werte', the turning upside down of all (known) values. At the heart of the text is an allusion to *Acts 17: 6*: 'these that have turned the world upside down have come hither also' (AV) . Peter Cutts (b. 1937) wrote a tune specially for it, which is included in *Pilgrim Praise*, for which fellow-hymnwriter David Goodall suggested the name ST. OMEGALPH (!).

102 The love of God is broad

11.10.11.10.
and chorus 11.10.

The love of God is broad like beach and meadow,
wide as the wind, and an eternal home.
God leaves us free to seek him or reject him,
he gives us room to answer 'yes' or 'no'.
The love of God is broad like beach and meadow,
wide as the wind, and an eternal home.

We long for freedom where our truest being
is given hope and courage to unfold.
We seek in freedom space and scope for dreaming,
and look for ground where trees and plants can grow.
Chorus

But there are walls that keep us all divided;
we fence each other in with hate and war.
Fear is the bricks-and-mortar of our prison,
our pride of self the prison coat we wear.
Chorus

O, judge us, Lord, and in your judgment free us,
and set our feet in freedom's open space;
take us as far as your compassion wanders
among the children of the human race.
Chorus

This is one of the most successful contemporary hymns to have flowed from the pen of Anders Frostenson. It has become extremely popular in the Scandinavian countries, in Germany, and - more slowly - in the English-speaking world. I translated it for the fourth edition of *Cantate Domino*. The melody GUDS KÄRLEK to which this text is firmly wedded is by the Swedish composer Lars Åke Lundberg, and is also found in *Songs and Hymns from Sweden*.

119

103 Blues for the Church

The trouble with many of our churches
is that they are not singing the blues.
The trouble with its staunch belongers
is the detached way they watch the news.
The trouble with our Sunday buildings
is people staying glued to their pews.

The problem with religious people ?
They can't read graffiti on the wall,
they argue finer point of dogma,
their ears are too full to hear the Call.
The problem with those holy people
is that they are too sure they won't fall.

So many males, mitred in splendour,
are stifling their passion like a yawn,
telling peace-makers they should 'cool it',
huddling in prayer while earth is going-gone.
The holy people in procession
are leading (having) us on and on and on and on . . . .

No wonder Christ wept for the city,
over the rulers and Pharisees,
he sings the blues of love and struggle:
'If only you knew the way of peace'.
He still calls his people to follow,
to fight against death and make a feast!

This is the most recent text in this anthology, written in November 1983. It was triggered off by a postscript to a letter I received from one of my fellow-moderators, the Rev. Tony Burnham, of the North West Province of the United Reformed Church in the United Kingdom. He wrote: 'I believe that what's wrong with our churches, is that they don't sing the blues'. Tony Burnham and I, together with another of the twelve URC moderators, share a keen interest in jazz; all three of us are members of Ronnie Scott's jazz-club in London. At the time of writing, no tune has as yet been composed for it, but American jazz-pianist and singer Louise Rose is working on it.

104 The wall is down

9.8.9.8.

The wall is down, for Christ destroyed it;
no longer strangers, we are one.
The earth is round, so let's enjoy it
and join the circle with the Son.

The wall is down, for Christ created
a single people, ruled by peace;
where love is found and hate defeated.
the world becomes an open house.

The wall is down, but strong foundations
are laid for newness, life in hope:
a house of prayer for all the nations,
providing room for growing up.

The wall is down, the Lord of Easter
rebuilds the temple in three days,
and life becomes a time of feasting;
the scene is set for boundless praise.

At the 1974 North American Area Council of the World Alliance of Reformed Churches, in Stony Point, New York, Bible studies were led by Dr. Philip Potter, the then general secretary of the World Council of Churches. One of his Bible study lectures so inspired me, that I wrote the hymn while he was speaking, and I was able to hand him the completed text as he left the meeting room.

Dr. Potter's wife, Doreen, wrote a melody for it for our 1975 collection *Break Not the Circle*. The tune is called STONY POINT. Ron Klusmeier wrote his own new tune for this text, and included it on an LP (Kari Records, Canada, KRK 10375).

105 They saw you as the local builder's son

10.10.10.10.

They saw you as the local builder's son,
and therefore out of house of prayer and town
they chased you, by your prophecy enraged,
into the darkness, to the mountain edge.

They did not see in you the nation's hope,
or see you take and drink the bitter cup.
They did not recognize the love divine
in you, who bore away our guilt and sin.

They did not see your hand in anguish curled,
your hand that heals, the hand that made the world.
They failed to see, when darkness came at noon,
that on the cross your saving work was done.

The time will come when everyone shall see:
your grace is like a stream that fills the sea.
You give us of your covenant the sign,
and in your wounds you heal all human pain.

Translated for *Cantate Domino* from Anders Frostenson's original Swedish text of 1962. The tune HANDS dates from 1933 and is by Verner Ahlberg. This text and the Ahlberg tune are also included in *Songs and Hymns from Sweden* and *Ecumenical Praise*.

106 A hymn on earth being fulfilled   6.6.6.6.

The whole earth is fulfilled
With God's forbearing mind,
full of a godly grace
and sympathy divine.

God's goodness is too great
for happiness alone,
it goes through deepest pain,
bred in our very bone.

It penetrates as seed
into the furrow's womb
because it does not leave
the sleepers in the tomb.

Because it does not rest
until the lost are found,
sky-wide, the world becomes
a fair and fruitful ground.

The stars above, sky-high,
are by this seed prepared,
as servants sent to reap
the mercy of the Lord.

The seed of godly love,
the Lord, the word of truth,
descends into the earth,
into the soil of death.

All you, in love with God,
who for his goodness wait,
the grain waves in the wind
as psalm-tunes in the night.

I translated this text for *Cantate Domino* from a 1970 Dutch original
by the Rev. Willem Barnard, one of the Netherlands' most prolific and
successful poet-theologians. The melody is by Frits Mehrtens who
wrote it in 1959. The hymn was written as an introit based on the
antiphon for the second Sunday after Easter: *Psalm 33: 5-6.*

107 A hymn for Easter

8.8.8.8.8 8.

They set out on their homeward road,
the two disciples lost and sad,
re-living still the episode
when all was lost and life made bad:
an ugly cross had been the end
of Christ the perfect man and friend.

A stranger joined them as they walked
that he their company might share;
he listened to them as they talked
of broken hope and great despair.
And then the stranger made reply
that Christ the Lord was bound to die.

He spoke of Moses and his days
of Egypt and the promised land,
recalled the prophets and their ways,
the leadings of the father-hand.
At journey's end, to food and rest,
they made him feel a welcome guest.

Invited in and honoured most
to take his place at table's head,
the stranger-guest became the host*
by saying grace and breaking bread.
Then suddenly they knew that Christ
had made their common meal a feast.

O Jesus, come again, we pray,
and share with us the things we do.
Be our companion on our way,
let Easter in our homes come true.
And let our life and work proclaim
the power of your living name.

*Host: One who entertains a stranger;
the consecrated bread in the sacrament.

This is - I confess it - an attempt at up-dating James Ashcroft Noble's nineteenth century hymn 'Lord Jesus, in the days of old two walked with Thee in waning light', which appears in *Congregational Praise* (No.628) to a tune, WYCH CROSS especially composed for it in 1947 by Erik Routley. This is included in *Pilgrim Praise*. Ron Klusmeier set it to his own music, including it on his latest LP *Look Beyond* (August 1983) on a new label, 'The Gentle Clowns' 3192.

108 A hymn for Sunday

11.10.11.10.

This is the day when light was first created,
symbol and gift of order and design.
In light is God's intention clearly stated;
the break of day reveals his loving mind.

This is the day of our complete surprising,
repeat of Easter: Christ has come to life!
Now is the feast of love's revolt and rising
against the rule of hell and death and grief.

We join to praise, with every race and nation,
the God who with mankind his Spirit shares;
strong wind of change and earth's illumination,
dispelling static thoughts and darkest fears.

This is the day of worship and of vision,
great birthday of the church in every land.
Let Christians all confess their sad division,
and seek the strength again as one to stand.

We pray that this, the day of re-creation,
may hallow all the week that is to come.
Help us, O Lord, to lay a good foundation
for all we do at work, at school, at home.

Written for the Pilgrim Church in 1966, this is a bundling-together
of all the reasons why we celebrate Sunday in worship: Creation,
the Resurrection, Pentecost. Originally sung to EASTWOOD by
Eric Shave (b. 1901). In the 1972 edition of *Pilgrim Praise*,
STRENGTH AND STAY (J. B. Dykes, 1823 - 76) is suggested.

109 Time is full to overflowing

8.7.8.5.

Time is full to overflowing,
trees are newly dressed in green.
Through the land the news is spreading:
God will come to reign.

In the hope to know tomorrow,
eyes are turned to scan the sky,
terrified by night and lightning,
storm and raging tide.

Day is nearing when the nations
will be tested for their worth.
Watch and pray against temptation;
all will be unearthed.

He, the Judge, who is our gladness,
now is standing at the door:
Jesus will be born of woman,
Jesus will be Lord.

See him hour by hour advancing,
marching through the Christian year;
He whom clouds will bear to heaven,
Christ, the man, is here.

In our hands he lays the tokens,
royal gifts of bread and wine,
raising us to life eternal
out of death's domain.

No-one knows the days and seasons
when the kingdom is to come;
build as if it came tomorrow,
be awake, make room!

A translation from Swedish of Lars Thunberg's 1968 text 'Tidens mått har fyllts till randen', with a melody FULL TO OVERFLOWING by Ingmar Milveden (1970), this appears in *Songs and Hymns from Sweden*. Written for Advent, the biblical references for this text are *Luke 21: 29* (v.1); *Luke 21: 25* (v.2); *Luke 21: 35* (v.3); and *Matthew 24: 30-36* (vv.4-7).

110 A hymn in the first person singular

10.11.10.11.

Today I live, but once shall come my death;
one day shall still my laughter and my crying,
bring to a halt my heart-beat and my breath:
Lord, give me faith for living and for dying.

How I shall die, or when, I do not know,
nor where, for endless is the world's horizon;
but save me, Lord, from thoughts that lay me low,
from morbid fears that freeze my power of reason.

When earthly life shall close, as close it must,
let Jesus be my brother and my merit.
Let me without regret recall the past,
then, Lord, into your hands commit my spirit.

Meanwhile I live and move and I am glad,
enjoy this life and all its interweaving;
each given day, as I take up the thread,
let love suggest my mode, my mood of living.

The subject of this hymn was suggested by my wife, Elly, who once commented how few hymns there are about death and dying. I called it 'A hymn in the first person singular', as it is a rather personal statement on this issue, but also because dying is an experience through which everyone has to pass individually. Included in *Break Not the Circle* it has been set to music by Doreen Potter; the tune is called BELLEGARDE. Ron Klusmeier also wrote a most sensitive tune for it, which is included on an LP (Kari Records, Canada, KRK 10375). In the *Hymnal Supplement* the set tune is HEARTBEAT by Jane Marshall.

Line 2 in verse 2 is a direct reference to the fact that at the time of writing I was on the staff of the Geneva-based World Alliance of Reformed Churches, and my work entailed a great deal of air travel - altogether some 500 flights with 80 different airlines in a ten-year span!

111 A hymn for Advent

7.6.7.6.D.

Tomorrow Christ is coming,
as yesterday he came;
a child is born this moment,
we do not know its name.
The world is full of darkness,
again there is no room;
the symbols of existence
are stable, cross and tomb.

Tomorrow will be Christmas,
the feast of love divine,
but for the nameless millions
the star will never shine.
Still is the census taken
with people on the move;
new infants born in stables
are crying out for love.

There will be no tomorrows
for many a baby born.
Good Friday falls on Christmas
when life is sown as corn.
But Jesus Christ is risen
and comes again in bread
to still our deepest hunger
and raise us from the dead.

Our Lord becomes incarnate
in every human birth.
Created in his image
we *must* make peace on earth.
God will fulfil his purpose
and this shall be the sign:
we shall find Christ among us
as woman, child or man.

Written for Advent, and submitted to Southern Television in a 'Hymn for Britain' competition in 1966, originally with a tune by Philip Humphreys, who was a curate at St. Andrew's Church of England in Plymouth. Later included in *Pilgrim Praise* to AU FORT DE MA DETRESSE (*French Psalter*, 1542) this text became popular in Canada when it appeared in the *Canadian Hymnbook*, to the tune LITTLE BADDOW by Cecil Armstrong Gibbs (1889 - 1960). Earlier, in 1972, this text had been published in the 1972 full music edition of *Pilgrim Praise* to a melody L'AVENT composed by Doreen Potter.

In the original text, there was a fifth verse, which was omitted from the later editions:

> We must go out to meet him
> — and we must do it now —.
> With gifts of time and talent
> let us before him bow.
> Then, on our way rejoicing
> for what we've seen and heard,
> we give our hearts to all men
> to prove that Christ is Lord!

112 A hymn for the close of worship

6.6.6.6.8 8.

To show by touch and word
devotion to the earth;
to hold in full regard
all life that comes to birth,
we need, O Lord, the will to find
the good you had of old in mind.

Lord, give us minds to choose
the things that matter most,
and hearts that long for truth
till pride-of-self is lost.
For every challenge that we face
we need your guidance and your grace.

Let love from day to day
be yardstick, rule and norm,
and let our lives portray
your word in human form.
Now come with us, that we may have
your wits about us where we live.

'A hymn for the close of worship', written for *Break Not the Circle*. Again, as with so many of my hymns, the text stresses the tension point of translating worship into the service of our week-day existence and behaviour. Compare the last line of verse 1 with the recurring phrase in *Genesis 1*, 'Behold, it was good'. Note in the last line of verse 3 we do not live by our own wits, but by the wits (logos ?) of our Lord. The tune ERLEY was composed for it by Doreen Potter. Ron Klusmeier wrote another tune for it which came out on the LP *Ron and Kris and Fred and Walter* (Kari Records, Canada, KRK 10375).

113 To work and live for others

To love our sisters, brothers,
it is our solemn vow,
but all is vanished now
in our neglect of others.
Our weakness needs forgiving;
we need new hearts for living.
Ourselves to life committing,
our life for service fitting,
we make a vow for living:
ourselves to others giving.

Then let us be committed,
resolved to do the right,
against injustice fight,
to speak the truth in love,
towards each other move.
Chorus

Translated from an original Bengali text for the collection of songs from urban settings in Asia, *New Songs of Asian Cities*. The music SOLEMN VOW to go with this text is by Suhas Sarkar of India.

114 A hymn of affluence and poverty

8.7.8.7.7 7.

Wealthy man, you are imprisoned,
riches are your cell and chain;
by your selfish will arrested,
trapped by your pursuit of gain.
Lazarus, who once was poor,
lives with God and dies no more.

To the man, at banquet's doorway,
after years of need and shame,
holy angels came and carried
him to be with Abraham.
But the man, who did so well
is rejected now in hell.

If not in the human conscience
God's redeeming work is done,
owners soon become possession
of the things they gained and won.
All who freedom's gift deny
unremembered they will die.

For the God of great creations,
who is wealthiest of all,
in the likeness of a poor man,
whom the people caused to fall,
he has made the world to see
how we can be truly free.

He came down to servant level,
sharing people's need and stress,
and his kingly coming gave to
poverty its righteousness.
But appearances of gain
will dissolve in loss and pain.

Translation of a Willem Barnard hymn, 'Rijke man, gij zit gevangen', based on *Luke 16: 19-31*, the Gospel for the first Sunday after Trinity (in the Anglican tradition). We sang it to ST. LEONARD (Johann Christoph Bach, 1642 - 1703) when Dr. Barnard was the guest preacher at the Pilgrim Church, Plymouth, in 1965.

Under the title 'A hymn of affluence and poverty', this hymn appears in the 1972 edition of *Pilgrim Praise* to the tune GOTT DES HIMMELS by Heinrich Albert (1604 - 51).

115 An uneasy carol

11.10.11.10.

We come uneasy, Lord, this festive season,
afraid that all may be just as before;
so hallow, help us use, each restive reason
that makes us want to see through tale and lore.

We come uneasy, longing to be able
to look beyond the symbols and the signs,
to find behind our carols and the bible
the living Word, as read between the lines.

We come uneasy, asking for your leading
to take our distance from the manger-scene
and go into our mainstreets for our reading
of all that can in people's eyes be seen.

We come, uneasy at the thought of knowing
the child who suffers, all who die too soon:
you, present-Lord, in human likeness growing
from cradle of the night to cross at noon.

We welcome you, uneasy at your coming,
but reassured that you have come to stay
to bind together your and our becoming
a sign of hope, a light to save the day.

Then free us from traditions that diminish
the glory of your Christmas to a farce.
Make good our will, from yearly start to finish,
to *'see* this thing that (daily) comes to pass'.

'An uneasy carol' owes its origin to things three of my ministers in
the West Midlands Province of the United Reformed Church said or
wrote during the days of Advent 1980: The Revs. Ivor Howells of
Dudley, Graham Spicer of West Bromwich and Brian Nutall of
Coventry. It was first published in the October issue of *The Hymn*,
the quarterly journal of the Hymn Society of America, 1981
(Volume 32, Number 4). Suggested tunes are INTERCESSOR by
Hubert Parry or CITY OF GOD by Daniel Moe.

116 A hymn on Christian unity

10 10.10 10.

We dare not, Father, ask to be as one,
if we are not united with your Son;
then stir us up each day to make request
that we in life may have the mind of Christ.

We cannot hope for Christians to be one
without the will to see that right is done.
Make us with pain of worldly needs aware;
teach us to love the people as they are.

We dare to ask that you will guide us first
to waste no longer things we hold in trust;
Lord, set us free from all that ties us down
and lead your church into the great unknown.

I wrote this for the Week of Prayer for Christian Unity in January 1968, to the tune CHILTON FOLIAT, by George Clement Martin (1844 - 1916). The full music edition of *Pilgrim Praise* suggests ELLERS by Edward John Hopkins (1818 - 1901), as well as a tune ONE IN CHRIST specially composed for it by H. W. Holmsen.

117 A hymn for Palm Sunday and Easter

We have a king who rides a donkey,
and his name is Jesus:
Jesus the king is risen
early in the morning.

Trees are waving a royal welcome
for the king called Jesus:
Chorus

We have a king who cares for people,
and his name is Jesus:
Chorus

A loaf and a cup upon the table,
bread-and-wine is Jesus:
Chorus

We have a king with a bowl and towel,
servant-king is Jesus:
Chorus

What shall we do with our life this morning?
give it up in service!

'A hymn for Palm Sunday and Easter', written for a family service at the
Pilgrim Church in 1968, to the tune, unashamedly, of WHAT SHALL
WE DO WITH THE DRUNKEN SAILOR?, bearing in mind that when
the disciples preached the Easter Gospel on the first day of Pentecost,
the crowds in Jerusalem thought they were drunk! This is in the 1972
edition of *Pilgrim Praise*.

118 Celebrating God's reign

We long to learn to praise,
in silence and with tone;
to worship you in many ways,
together and alone.
Lord, teach us where and how
to celebrate your reign,
with all the things that come to hand,
in colour and design.

Let worship come to life
in humble frame of mind,
in our approach to people, things,
and in our use of time.
Lord, you desire our praise
in actions planned and done.
through workmanship in daily task,
in leisure time and fun.

Give us your lines to learn
and prompt us in our role
of being one with all who live,
to love with heart and soul.
Help us to live and sing
the truly human sound;
from church to world, at home, at work,
in one unbroken round.

Written specially for a worship service at the ecumenical centre in Geneva in 1971, with a melody LA FEUILASSE composed for it by Doreen Potter. It is also sung to ICH HALTE TREULICH STILL, attributed to J. S. Bach. First published in the 1972 edition of *Pilgrim Praise.*

119 The tree springs to life

5.5.5.5.6.5.6.5.
or 10 10. 11 11.

We meet you, O Christ.
in many a guise;
your image we see
in simple and wise.
You live in a palace,
exist in a shack.
We see you, the gardener,
a tree on your back.

In millions alive,
away and abroad,
involved in our life
you live down the road.
Imprisoned in systems
you long to be free.
We see you, Lord Jesus,
still bearing your tree.

We hear you, O Man,
in agony cry.
For freedom you march,
in riots you die.
Your face in the papers
we read and we see.
The tree must be planted
by human decree.

You choose to be made
at one with the earth;
the dark of the grave
prepares for your birth.
Your death is your rising,
creative your word:
the tree springs to life
and our hope is restored!

This text was born when I was preparing the script for a BBC television programme in the series 'Seeing and Believing' in 1966. The programme was broadcast on Passion Sunday that year, when it coincided with the 25th anniversary of the destruction of the city of Plymouth in a German air raid. The theme caption for the programme (which was called 'The Tree Springs to Life') was a photograph of the bombed church of Saint Andrew's, where out of a heap of stones and rubble in the nave, a small apple tree had miraculously pushed its way through and was in blossom.

It was sung in the broadcast by the folksinger Len Pearcy, to a melody FREEDOM FIELDS by Philip Humphreys, curate at St. Andrew's at the time. Later, other tunes were composed for it, notably one by Erik Routley, DURHAM 72 for the book *Ecumenical Praise*. Ron Klusmeier included it in his LP *Thank you that now is the time of our life* (Vintage Records, Canada, SCV 132), but the most exciting melody for it is probably the one Pablo Sosa, of Argentina, wrote for it, for the worship book of the World Conference on World Mission and Evangelism in Melbourne, 1980. The melody is called BOSSEY.

120 Jesus Christ—the life of the world

7.6.7.6.
and chorus 3.5.

We need to breathe, for living
with body, soul and mind,
the presence of the Spirit,
the promises of Christ.
Jesus Christ –
the life of the world!

For living we must suffer
all that reduces life,
with Christ arise and conquer
the things that are of death.
Chorus

God's people need for living
to grow 'till Kingdom come',
grow up into its fullness,
all-varied and yet one.
Chorus

All living must be striving
to love whom God has made,
and breaking down divisions
where Jesus leads the way.
Chorus

This is my bid for an English translation from the German original by Dieter Trautwein, who wrote it for the 1983 Assembly of the World Council of Churches in Vancouver. My translation was eventually turned down by the Assembly music committee, in favour of one by Canadian musician and choirleader Len Lythgoe. The melody VANCOUVER 1983 to which this text is intended is one by Herbert Beuerle, of the Federal Republic of Germany.

121 A hymn for a dedication or anniversary of a church

11.10.11.10.

We praise your name, O God of all creation,
for making plain the purpose of your will;
we thank you for creative inspiration
and our responding through design and skill.

We thank you that our faith has found expression
in walls that shelter those who worship here;
help us to be a house of intercession
and make us glad the world is ever near.

We set this place apart for praise and preaching,
for breaking bread and practice to forgive;
we pray that through the humbleness of teaching
together, young and old may learn to live.

Keep free our life from bondage of tradition
and let your Holy Spirit set the trend;
endow us with an urgent sense of mission;
our doors be wide to welcome and to send.

Your word be in our actions clearly spoken,
extend our church beyond the builder's plan;
and use our witness as a vivid token
that you are still *with* woman, child and man.

This hymn was commissioned by the Rev. Keith Forecast for the official opening of Derriford Congregational (now United Reformed) Church in Plymouth in 1967. It was first sung to CHARTERHOUSE by David Evans (1874 - 1948). In the 1972 edition of *Pilgrim Praise* it is suggested to ZU MEINEM HERRN by Johann Gottfried Schicht (1753 - 1823), and to a new tune NOTT specially composed by Alan Ridout.

122 Worship and practical praise

10 10. 11 11.
or 5.5.5.5.6.5.6.5.

We rise to respond
— with common accord —
confronted by him
who gives us his Word.
His truth is for doing,
by him we are moved
and called to interpret
the meaning of love.

He calls us to build
a city on earth,
where love will surround
each person from birth.
He calls us and sends us
to be of mankind,
to share with the living
his bread and his wine.

Then let us accept
the terms of our brief:
to work and to love
and give of our life,
that, newly committed
to Christ and his ways,
our life may be worship
and practical praise.

*If the following alternative to the last verse is sung, it is suggested that
the congregation leave the church while singing it:*

We rise to translate
our praise into deed;
prepared to go out,
we follow God's lead.
From Sunday to Monday
the challenge remains:
when worship is over,
the service begins.

Like the previous hymn, this one was commissioned by my colleague Rev. Keith Forecast for his induction service as minister of Roath Park Congregational Church, Cardiff, 1970. I wrote the fourth, alternative last verse much later, for an act of worship at the ecumenical centre, Geneva, when the worshippers actually left the chapel as they were still singing that verse. Doreen Potter wrote a tune ST. KATHERINE specially for that occasion. It is popularly sung these days to HANOVER by William Croft (1678 - 1727), which is in *Pilgrim Praise.*

123 A new hymn for worship

11.10.11.10.

We tingle with excitement at the knowledge
that God is love: the Easter-news is true!
We wait upon the prompting of the Spirit
in all the things our talents find to do.

*We make response in reaching out to others,
in striving for the quality of life
and care by which our God is truly honoured;
we celebrate in *kind* the gift of life.

With holiness and beauty on our palette,
we 'paint the town' in every hue of praise
and write our poetry of hope and longing,
with love and laughter decorate our days.

We raise the roof of cellar and cathedral
with sounds of jazz, with symphony and song,
and pray that in our practice and our playing
the consonance with heaven may be strong.

How can our hands be still, our feet be idle
through dance and music, colour and design,
invited by the Man who comes, proclaiming
the Gloria of water changed to wine?

Let all the world weave tapestries of worship
to God, creation's origin and crown;
to Christ, the life and soul of Cana's party;
and to the Spirit of the festive round.

*Lord, you elude all human formulations,
your majesty exceeds our schemes of thought:
so make us in our worship humbly joyful
and in our witness willing to be taught.

* *These verses may be omitted.*

© 1985 Hope Publishing Company for USA and Canada and Stainer & Bell Ltd
for other territories

I was one of five hymnwriters around the world, who were commissioned by the American Lutheran Church to write a new hymn for worship to mark the 500th anniversary of the birth and baptism of Martin Luther (1483 - 1546). The hymn was to express 'the joy of worship/witness as related to the arts'. The American composer, Calvin Hampton, who has set several of my texts to music, was commissioned to write a melody KAAN for this text, which was then first sung at a Festival of Worship and Witness in Minneapolis, USA, June 1983.

124 The family of nations

11.10.11.10.

We turn to you, O God of every nation,
giver of life and origin of good;
your love is at the heart of all creation,
your hurt is people's broken brotherhood.

We turn to you that we may be forgiven
for crucifying Christ on earth again.
We know that we have never wholly striven
to share with all the promise of your reign.

Free every heart from pride and self-reliance,
our ways of thought inspire with simple grace;
break down among us barriers of defiance,
speak to the soul of all the human race.

On all who fight on earth for right relations
we pray the light of love from hour to hour.
Grant wisdom to the leaders of the nations,
the gift of carefulness to those in power.

Teach us, good Lord, to serve the need of others,
help us to give and not to count the cost.
Unite us, help us live as sisters, brothers,
defeat our Babel with your Pentecost!

This is a hymn for United Nations Day, 24th October, written for the Pilgrim Church in Plymouth in 1965. We first sang it to INTERCESSOR by Charles Hubert Hastings Parry (1848 - 1918). The first denominational hymnbook to take up this text was the supplement to *Hymns Ancient and Modern, 100 Hymns for Today* followed by *Hymns and Songs* and the *New Catholic Hymnal*. Since then it has been impossible to keep track of the number of occasions on which it has been incorporated in hymnals and orders of service. In *Pilgrim Praise* the LONDONDERRY AIR is set to this text.

125 A hymn on life and peace

10 10.11 11.

We utter our cry: that peace may prevail!
That earth will survive and faith must not fail.
We pray with our life for the world in our care,
for people diminished by doubt and despair.

We cry from the fright of our daily scene
for strength to say 'No' to all that is mean:
designs bearing chaos, extinction of life,
all energy wasted on weapons of death.

We lift up our hearts for children unborn:
give wisdom, O God, that we may hand on,
re-plenished and tended, this good planet earth,
preserving the future and wonder of birth.

Creator of life, come, share out, we pray,
your Spirit on earth, revealing the Way
to statesmen conferring 'round tables for peace,
that they may from bias and guile be released.

Come with us, Lord-Love, in protest and march,
and help us to fire with passion your church,
to match all our statements and lofty resolve
with being – unresting – in action involved.

Whatever the ill or pressure we face,
Lord, hearten and heal, give insight and grace
to think and make peace with each heartbeat and breath,
choose Christ before Caesar and life before death!

As I was about to leave for a fortnight's holiday in Cuba, in February 1983, I received a telephone call from Olle Dahlen, Swedish ambassador to the United Nations, asking me if I would write a hymn for the opening service of a Christian World Conference on Life and Peace. The text came into being while I was in Cuba, and on my return I sent it to Sweden, where it was warmly accepted. I was subsequently invited to attend the conference as a delegate, and so was present in Uppsala Cathedral on 20th April, when it was sung by a congregation of several thousand people. The hymn was sung several times during the Conference, and was finally included in the official Message which the delegates agreed upon on 23rd April. The tune to which it was sung, for 'easy access', was HANOVER by William Croft (1678 - 1727) which is included in the *Hymnal Supplement*. Sixty-two countries were represented at the Conference.

In February 1985 this hymn, with a new tune UPPSALA specially composed for it by Peter Cutts (b. 1937), was one of the eight winning entries in a BBC hymn-writing competition for the television programme 'Songs of Praise Festival 1985'.

126 Let all the world blossom

7.7.7.7.7.7.10.

We who bear the human name
are like flowers of the field;
without status, without fame,
trampled down and made to yield,
unprotected and exposed
to the scorching wind that blows.
Let all the world now blossom as a field!

Even Solomon of old,
(said our Lord, the Man of peace)
with his glory and his gold
could not match the flowers' grace.
We are weak but we recall
how the mighty ones must fall.
Let all the world now blossom as a field!

We are people of the field,
crowding Asia's city streets.
We are people called to build
a community of peace.
We remember as we toil
hope is springing from the soil.
Let all the world now blossom as a field!

This is perhaps the most international sample of hymn-writing. When I was in Jakarta, Indonesia, as text consultant to the editor of *New Songs for Asian Cities*, in 1972, I was one morning at breakfast presented with a paper serviette on which Professor Masao Takenaka, of Doshisha University, Japan, had scribbled a few Japanese characters, with an English translation. He asked me if I would work these ideas out into a hymn - which I did there and then. Subsequently, it was necessary for the editor, Professor I-to Loh, of Tainan Theological Seminary, to find a suitable tune for it. He came up with a children's song from Indonesia, a pedicab driver's song. So now, in *New Songs of Asian Cities*, we have a hymn written in English by a Dutchman to an idea by a Japanese, sung to an Indonesian tune discovered by a Taiwanese! The tune title suggested is CHILDREN OF INDONESIA.

127 A hymn on reconciliation 11.11.11.5.

When any person is to Christ united,
the past is gone, the present is re-stated.
How shall we live, to God's new world related?
Love will dictate it.

At peace with God, in love with those around us,
we are set free from all that cramped and bound us;
by love constrained, we give ourselves to others:
sisters and brothers.

In the new order, we are called to service,
sent in the name of Him whose nature love is,
proclaiming to the world by rhyme and reason:
Jesus is risen.

I wrote this hymn, based on *2 Corinthians 5*, for the Uniting Assembly
of the International Congregational Council and the World Presbyterian
Alliance, which took place in Nairobi, Kenya, 20th - 30th August 1970.
In the full music edition of *Pilgrim Praise*, ROUEN is suggested, an
eighteenth century French church melody.

128 A hymn on freedom in service   6.5.6.5.D.

When in his own image
God made humankind,
he enfolded freedom
in his great design.
For he loved us even
from before our birth;
granting us dominion
of our planet earth.

God entrusted to us
life as gift and aim.
Sin became our prison,
turning hope to shame.
Cain against his brother
lifted hand and sword,
and the Father's pleading
went unseen, unheard.

Then in time, our Maker
chose to intervene,
set his love in person
in the human scene.
Jesus broke the circle
of repeated sin,
so that our devotion
newly might begin.

Choose we now in freedom
where we should belong,
let us turn to Jesus,
let our choice be strong.
May the great obedience
which in Christ we see
perfect all our service:
then we shall be free!

God created man - went the original opening line. Revised, it goes like this:

> When in his own image
> God made humankind,

Originally written for the Pilgrim Church, and published in *Pilgrim Praise*, this hymn was incorporated in preparatory documentation that was sent out for the 5th Assembly of the World Council of Churches in Nairobi in 1975. The hymn was translated into several languages for that purpose. It was also incorporated in *Cantate Domino*, to a tune specially composed for it by James Carley, then Professor of Church Music at the Disciples of Christ Theological Seminary, Indianapolis, USA.

129 When Jesus sat down at the lakeshore

9.8.9.8.9.10.

When Jesus sat down at the lakeshore,
the people flocked round him to hear.
The surf, and the wind from the mountains,
they carried his words to their ears,
of sowing and fishing and treasures:
and all is nearness and wind from afar.

When Jesus sat down at the wellside,
a woman came out from the town,
rejected by public opinion
because of her doubtful renown;
but Jesus returned her to living:
and all is nearness and streams from afar.

When Jesus sat down in the desert,
they brought to him those who were ill.
He healed their despair and diseases:
'Arise and go home, you are well!'
And then he broke bread with the hungry:
and all is nearness and strength from afar.

And now he is with us for ever:
he sits at the Father's right hand;
he serves us at table, we meet him
in city streets and on the land.
His word is our hope and our challenge:
and all is nearness, for his is the world.

Translated for *Cantate Domino* from a Swedish original by Anders Frostenson, to a melody AT THE LAKESHORE by Roland Forsberg, it can also be found in *Songs and Hymns from Sweden*. Biblical references are: *Matthew 13: 1ff* (v.1); *John 4: 6* (v.2); *Mark 2: 1ff* (v.3); *Hebrews 8: 1* (v.4).

130 The colourful year

7 8.7 8.

When Noah's ark was high and dry,
there came a rainbow in the sky
and Noah heard a voice divine:
'I am your God and you are mine'.

This God, who ever faithful stays,
has given colour to our days.
The shade with which the year begins
is purple for the people's sins.

On Christmas-day we see the light,
— the colour of the feast is white —
and when the Kings have left the scene,
our life runs into days of green.

In Lent to purple we go back,
and on Good Friday all is black.
But sorrow is not meant to stay,
proclaims the white of Easter-day!

As red as flames of Pentecost,
so is the blood the martyrs lost.
Then, till the hopeful Advent sound,
we make with green the circle round.

The church from day to day is led
through purple, black and green and red,
from fasting times to days of feast,
from black of sin to white of Christ!

One of very few children's hymns I have written. It arose when for the Pilgrim Church in Plymouth I designed a set of pulpit and lectern hangings in the liturgical colours. As the use of liturgical colours is not all that prevalent in the Free Churches, I wrote this text for the children of the church in order to teach them the sequences of the Christian year and the colours we use to symbolise the various seasons. We sang it to TRURO, from *Psalmodia Evangelica*, 1789, but the full music edition of *Pilgrim Praise* also offers a new tune MARRIOTT written specially for this text by Alan Ridout.

131 A world full of people

9.8.9.8.

While still the world is full of people,
and mother-earth her increase gives,
we give our thanks to you, the Keeper
and Father God of all that lives.

As long as human words are spoken
and for each other we exist,
you give your love as faithful token,
we thank you in the name of Christ.

You feed the birds in tree and rafter,
you clothe the flowers in the field.
You shelter us now and hereafter,
and to your care our days we yield.

You are our light and our salvation,
you raise your people from the dead.
You gave your Son for every nation,
his body is the living bread.

The world is bound to bow before you,
you brought it by your love to birth,
you live among us, we adore you,
we are your children down-to-earth.

Translation of an immensely popular Dutch hymn of Huub Oosterhuis,
a Jesuit priest and minister of the student 'ecclesia' at Amsterdam
University. 'Zo lang er mensen zijn op aarde' written in 1958,
was incorporated in *Cantate Domino* to the tune to which it has
become firmly wedded in Dutch worship, one composed by
Tera de Marez Oyens-Wansink (1959). In *Pilgrim Praise* it appears with
LES COMMANDEMENS DE DIEU (*Genevan Psalter*, 1549 - 51).

132 Not so much a hymn (2)

7 7.6.7 7.8.

With fervent dedication,
in talks and consultation,
we prostitute the word.
Conferring round the table,
(a long way from that stable),
we sit and serve the servant-Lord.

While people starve in cities,
we travel to committees
until the kingdom come.
We share a high allegiance,
divide the world in regions;
departments are our second home.

At one with all the needy
in document and study,
we live the human plight.
Amidst the death of laughter,
we praise the great hereafter
while Jesus walks our streets of fright.

Lord, shame us out of talking,
teach us the art of walking
as far as we can go.
Show us new ways of caring,
with all your people sharing
the hope we have, the love we owe.

The second of two texts entitled 'Not so much a hymn'. I wrote it while working in Geneva, and - more specifically - I wrote it during a verbose and boring committee meeting. Almost tongue-in-cheek, it has been sung to INNSBRUCK by Heinrich Isaak (1460 - 1527) as harmonised by J. S. Bach. Ron Klusmeier has set this text to a tune which is included on the LP *Look Beyond* (The Gentle Clown Records 3192). On the record sleeve, this text is entitled, 'The Committee Song'. *Pilgrim Praise* also suggests TUPPER by Alan Ridout.

133 A hymn for baptism (3)

9.8.9.8.

With grateful hearts our faith professing,
we ask you, Lord, come to our aid,
that we, our children re-possessing,
may keep the vows that we have made.

We know that in your true providing
the young and old to Christ belong;
Lord, help us to be wise in guiding,
and make us in example strong.

Give to the parents love and patience,
each home with Christian graces fill,
protect our children in temptations,
and keep them safe in childhood's ill.

Accept, O Lord, our dedication
to fill with love the growing mind,
that in this church and congregation
the young a faith for life may find.

This is an early *Pilgrim Praise* hymn, written in 1963 or 1964, and sung to LES COMMENDEMENS DE DIEU from the *Genevan Psalter*. It can also be sung to ST. CLEMENT by C. C. Scholefield. Although intended for a baptismal service, the hymn has a wider challenge to all those responsible for the upbringing of children. The idea for the last line came to me as a result of my involvement with Westward Television, Plymouth, for whom I was a regular contributor to epilogue programmes, which were known under the title 'Faith for Life'.

134 An evening hymn

8 8.7.4 4.7.

You are on earth, Lord Jesus Christ,
of all the jewels that exist,
most precious for possession,
and every day,
– befall what may –
you are my heart's confession.

Of all that lives, on earth, above,
none can exceed your faithful love,
and I am well persuaded
that all of life
and even death
are by your love pervaded.

Your word is true, it cannot lie,
and on its promise I rely
in every day's endeavour.
Your word is true,
I turn to you;
your love will last for ever.

The day departs; to you, my Lord,
who are as faithful as your word,
I give myself for keeping.
Lord, let your light
be round me bright,
and guard my soul while sleeping.

Like No.62 in this anthology, this hymn was translated into English at the request of Dr. Bohumil Kejr, conductor of a Czech male voice choir on the occasion of their tour of England in 1969. 'Mein schönste Zier und Kleinod' originated in Leipzig in 1597, with a melody AM ABEND identified as coming from a Leipzig 1573/Nuremberg 1581 source. It is included in *Pilgrim Praise* to this tune.

135 You call and create from blindness and death the things that are

10.4.10.4.
and chorus
7.5.7.5.

You call and create from blindness and death
the things that are.
Your Word on its way, your Spirit released,
renew what is.
All that we have comes from you.
All your love comes true.
All that we have comes from you.
All your love comes true.

Your reign comes to light 'mid rubble and dust,
a treasure found.
The price of our life: your cross and your grave;
with you we rise.
Chorus

Creation is yours, its hurt is our call
to rise and serve.
From you we receive the gift we must lay
in hung'ring hands.
Chorus

'Du kaller på ting ur blindhet och död' was translated from a Swedish
original of Anders Frostenson with a Lars Åke Lundberg tune YOU
CALL AND CREATE (written and composed in 1969), for the
anthology *Songs and Hymns from Sweden*. Biblical references are given
as: *1 Corinthians 3: 21; Romans 4: 17* (v.1); *Psalm 104: 30* (v.2);
Psalm 24: 1 (v.3).

136 A hymn for confirmation

C.M.

1a You called me, Father, by my name
when I had still no say;
today you call me to confirm
the vows my parents made.

1b Lord, when I came into this life
you called me by my name;
today I come, commit myself,
responding to your claim.

2 You give me freedom to believe,
today I make my choice
and to the worship of the church
I add my learning voice.

3 Within the circle of the faith,
as member of your cast,
I take my place with all the saints
of future, present, past.

4 In all the tensions of my life,
between my faith and doubt,
let your great Spirit give me hope,
sustain me, lead me out.

5 So, help me in my unbelief
and let my life be true:
feet firmly planted on the earth,
my sights set high on you.

Verse 1b is offered as an alternative where a person has not been baptised in infancy. The hymn can also be sung in the first person plural.

When our younger son Peter was confirmed, I could not be present at the service, as I was in Canada at the time, doing a series of sing-along concerts and worship work-shops with Ron and Kris Klusmeier (whom I have mentioned before in these notes) and Canadian hymnwriter Walter Farquharson, in October 1976. So I wrote 'A hymn for confirmation' as an indication that I would at least be present in spirit. The hymn was not sung at the service, as Peter was confirmed in the National Protestant Church of Geneva (which worships in French!). However, the hymn was used when our other two children were confirmed: Alison, at the American Episcopal Church, Geneva, in November 1977, and Martin, at St. Ninian's United Reformed Church, Hull, England, in February 1978. The tune to which it was sung was ST. PETER by Alexander Robert Reinagle (1799 - 1877). In 1979 I sent the hymn in to the Hymn Society of America, when they asked three hymnwriters to submit an unpublished text. The well-known American composer, Alice Parker, set it to music, calling the tune HAWLEY. The hymn was sung at the 1980 Convocation of the Hymn Society of America in Princeton, New Jersey, at a Kaan-Hymn Festival. In the *Hymnal Supplement* the tune by Alice Parker was renamed CONFIRMATION.

137 A hymn on becoming who we are

10.11.10.6 6.

You lead us, Lord, with miracle and grace;
we follow in your train of thought and calling.
With you we move in hope from place to place,
    and practise what shall be,
    for you have set us free.

We give thanks for all we've seen and heard,
but also for your future, never fearing
to stay within the earshot of your Word;
    Word that divides, creates,
    unsettles and unites.

Lord, make us of your beck and call aware,
help us accept the cost of 'kingdom-living',
the risk of our becoming who we are:
    Lord, use our faith and doubt,
    unite us, lead us out.

Like the first hymn in this anthology, I wrote this text while attending the 1976 Assembly of the Indonesian Council of Churches in Salatiga on the island of Java. No tune has as yet been composed for it. I have dedicated this text to the Rev. Marion de Velder, former General Secretary of the Reformed Church of America.

138 You, Lord, who chose to share   6 6 6.5.

You, Lord, who chose to share
and shoulder our despair,
be where your people are,
in fear and darkness.

Lord, you who went before,
counting our sins no more,
peace to our hearts restore;
be with us always.

You, who with living bread
fill the earth far and wide,
each day this bread provide,
Christ, at our table.

Lord, you who went ahead
into a world of dread,
send us with peace and bread
to all your people.

I translated this from Olov Hartmann's Swedish text, written in 1968, 'Du som gick före oss'. The hymn was included in *Cantate Domino* and *Songs and Hymns from Sweden*, with the tune SHARE AND SHOULDER which has been associated with this text from the beginning. It was composed by Sven Erik Back in 1959.

139 You who through the city had to bear your cross

11 11.

You who through the city had to bear your cross,
come again, be with us in the rush hour noise.

Come and walk our pavements worn by passing years;
you will find your vineyard and your fields are here.

See your kingdom founded in the dust of day,
living faith embedded in our human pain.

Help us to remember night and day are yours:
all our hectic minutes and our lonely hours.

Speak into the movement of our daylight haste,
voice that can't be silent, word that can't be lost.

Speak in all the tensions of our working time,
raising up among us peace as gift and sign.

Yet another Anders Frostenson text, written in 1965, and translated for *Songs and Hymns from Sweden*. The melody BEAR YOUR CROSS is by Roland Forsberg, composed in 1970 and revised in 1974.

140 Litany V, from the WCC Nairobi worship book

L: Lord, you made the world and everything in it;
    you created the human race of one stock
    and gave us the earth for our possession.

P: **Break down the walls that separate us
    and unite us in a single body.**

L: Lord, we have been divisive in our thinking,
    in our speech, in our actions;
    we have classified and imprisoned one another;
    we have fenced each other out by hatred and prejudice.

P: **Break down the walls that separate us
    and unite us in a single body.**

L: Lord, you mean us to be a single people,
    ruled by peace, feasting in freedom,
    freed from injustice, truly human, men and women,
    responsible and responsive in the life we lead,
    the love we share, the relationships we create.

P: **Break down the walls that separate us
    and unite us in a single body.**

L: Lord, we shall need ever-new insights into the truth,
    awareness of your will for all humanity,
    courage to do what is right — even when it is not allowed —
    persistence in undermining unjust structures
    until they crumble into dust,
    grace to exercise a ministry of reconciliation.

P: **Break down the walls that separate us
    and unite us in a single body.**

L: Lord, share out among us the tongues of the Spirit,
that we may each burn with compassion
for all who hunger for freedom and human-ness;
that we may be doers of the Word
and so speak with credibility
about the wonderful things you have done.

L & P: **Lord, direct us in ways we do not yet discern
and equip us for the service of reconciliation
and liberation in your world.**

P: **Break down the walls that separate us
and unite us in a single body.**

The last text in this anthology is that of a litany, rather than that of a hymn, but because it gained wide popularity through having a tune unexpectedly composed for it, I thought it proper to include it in this collection. The text is one of several I wrote for the Worship Book of the 5th Assembly of the World Council of Churches, in Nairobi in 1975. Almost as soon as I arrived at the Assembly, to which I had been invited as an adviser on worship, I discovered to my surprise that German composer and pop-group leader Peter Janssens had set these words to exciting and catchy music; and with his group, the 'Gesangsorchester', he taught the delegates to sing it. It became - quite uncalculatedly - one of the top hits of the Assembly, and was sung over and over again, both in official sessions and on the many occasions when the delegates sang and danced into the early hours of the morning at those all-time-high celebrations which Peter Janssens led 'after hours'. The litany became the title song of a best-selling LP of Assembly music (Pietbiet Records 1024).

Topical index

THE CHRISTIAN YEAR

Advent
Christ is coming, Christ has come *11*
Come and be surprised, all nations *15*
Each year we sing with bated Christmas voice *23*
Sing we a song of high revolt (Magnificat Now!) *93*
Tomorrow Christ is coming *111*

Christmas
Come and be surprised, all nations *15*
Each year we sing with bated Christmas voice *23*
Our God has given his Son to the earth *85*
We come uneasy, Lord, this festive season *115*

Lent
Christ is crucified today *12*
They saw you as the local builder's son *105*
We meet you, O Christ *119*

Palm Sunday
God will, when he comes down to earth *47*
The trouble with many of our churches *103*
We have a king who rides a donkey *117*

Holy Week and Good Friday
Christ is crucified today *12*
Lord God, who on the Friday of creation *69*
Move me to crying *75*
We meet you, O Christ *119*

Easter
Christ is alive! *10*
Christ is risen *13*
Committed to Christ *18*
Each Sunday brings to mind again *22*
God's Word throughout the ages *44*
He's back in the land of the living *49*
How can creation's voice be still *50*
How many fruits we gain *51*
Jesus, shepherd of our souls *59 (2nd Sunday after Easter)*
Lord God, we seek your face *68 (5th after Easter – Rogation)*
The language of the Hebrews *101*
The wall is down, for Christ destroyed it *104*
The whole earth is fulfilled *106*
They set out on their homeward road *107*
This is the day when light was first created *108*

169

We have a king who rides a donkey *117*
We tingle with excitement *123*

Ascension
Although our Lord has left us *3*

Pentecost
Come, O Holy Spirit *17*
O Holy Spirit, hear us as we pray *83*
This is the day when light was first created *108*

Trinity
God is unique and one *40*
I throw my rejoicing like birds to the heavens *57*

Christian Year – General
Christ is crucified today *12*
Time is full to overflowing *109*
When Noah's ark was high and dry *130*

WORSHIP

Approach
Each morning with its newborn light *21*
Each Sunday brings to mind again *22*
Gathered here from many nations *33*
God is unique and one *40*
God of bible and tradition *42*
Let us our hearts and voices raise *62*
Lord, how majestic is your name *70*
Praise the Lord with joyful cry *89*
This is the day when light was first created *108*
We tingle with excitement *123*

Confession
Lord, confronted with your might *66*
Lord, do not hold yourself apart *67*
Out of our failure to create *87*

Gloria
As the glory of creation *4*
Glory and anguish to God in the height *34*
Glory to God in the highest *35*

The Word
As the glory of creation *4*
Christ is coming, Christ has come *11*
God of bible and tradition *42*
God the creator *45*
God who spoke in the beginning *46*
How can creation's voice be still *50*

170

Life could be good *64*
The great commandment of our Lord *100*

Thanksgiving
Now join we, to praise the creator *78*
Thank you, O Lord, for the time that is now *97*

Intercession
For the healing of the nations *32*
We turn to you, O God of every nation *124*

Baptism
Now in the name of him who sent *77*
Out of deep unordered water *86*
With grateful hearts our faith professing *133*

Confirmation
We rise to respond *122*
You called me, Father, by my name *136*

Communion
As we break the bread *5*
Bread, feeding people's hope *7*
Christ is alive *10*
Christ is coming, Christ has come *11*
Down to earth *20*
For the crowd of thousands *31*
If you have ears, then listen *54*
Let all who share one bread and cup *60*
Let Christian people practise praise and love *61*
Let us talents and tongues employ *63*
Move me to crying *75*
Raising our hands as a sign of rejoicing *90*
You, Lord, who chose to share *138*

Post-Communion
Father, who in Jesus found us *29*
Now let us from this table rise *79*

Close of Worship
Christian people, serve the Lord *9*
Father, who in Jesus found us *29*
Lord, as we rise to leave *65*
To show by touch and word *112*

Ordination and Induction
We rise to respond *122*

Church Anniversary
This is the day when light was first created *108*
We praise your name, O God of all creation *121*
You called me/us, Father, by my/our name *136*

172

173

Father, help your people *27*
God has set us free for freedom *39*
Help us accept each other *48*
Life could be good *64*
Our faults divide and hinder *84*
Sing we of the modern city *94*
We who bear the human name *126*

Human Rights
Break down the walls *140*
Each year we sing with bated Christmas voice *23*
For ourselves no longer living *30*
For the healing of the nations *32*
Raising our hands as a sign of rejoicing *90*
We dare not, Father, ask to be as one *116*

Justice
Each year we sing with bated Christmas voice *23*
For the healing of the nations *32*
He's back in the land of the living *49*
Modern people have cities for their home *74*
Raising our hands as a sign of rejoicing *90*
To love our sisters, brothers *113*

Kingdom
Establish, Lord, your kingdom *25*
Father, help your people *27*
God calls his people firm to stand *36*
God's kingdom is among us *43*
Time is full to overflowing *109*
We need to breathe, for living *120*
You lead us, Lord *137*
You who through the city had to bear your cross *139*

Leisure
We long to learn to praise *118*

Life!
Almond trees, renewed in bloom *2*
Christ is alive! *10*
Christ is risen *13*
Come, dare to be *16*
Establish, Lord, your kingdom *25*
Father, we long to be people more human *28*
God's word throughout the ages *44*
He's back in the land of the living *49*
How wide is life for living *52*
Lord God, who on the Friday of creation *69*
Now let us translate in the language of human-ness *80*
See how swarming birds of heaven *91*

177

Metrical index

Acknowledgements

The Author and Publishers gratefully acknowledge the assistance of the following in allowing reproduction of copyright material in the introductory notes:

Dr. Norman Goodall and the Berean Press for quotations from *I believe in words*; Dr. Carlton R. Young and The Hymn Society of America for a quotation from the Society's quarterly journal; W. H. Allen & Co. and Doubleday & Company for quotations from *Music is my Mistress* by Duke Ellington, Copyright 1973 by Duke Ellington Inc.; Dr. Norman Goodall for a quotation from an address given to the London Society for the Study of Religion; the World Council of Churches for material in *Risk* by Albert van den Heuvel; to Geoffrey Chapman, a division of Cassell Ltd for extracts from *Theology in Reconciliation* by Thomas F. Torrance; to Rev. Dr. Fred Pratt Green and the Hymn Society of Great Britain for material from an address given to the Society; to Ron Klusmeier, PO Box 100, Cascade, Wisconsin 53011, USA for a quotation from the sleeve of *Look Beyond*.

The Author and Publishers also thank the following copyright owners for permission to include copyright material in the footnotes to the hymns: Punch Publications Limited; the United Reformed Church for material from *New Church Praise* Commentary; the Oxford and Cambridge University Presses for material from *New English Bible*, Second Edition, Copyright 1970; Eyre & Spottiswoode, Her Majesty's Printers, for extracts from the Authorized King James Version of the Bible, which is Crown Copyright in the United Kingdom; to Stanley Osborne for a brief quotation in the notes to hymn No.40.

The Author is also grateful for permission received to translate and paraphrase material written originally other than in the English tongue: in one or two instances, every effort to trace an original author has failed although the source is acknowledged in the text.

If despite every care having been taken, any copyright material is not acknowledged, the Publishers and Author apologise to those concerned and will correct the position in any future edition.

Further Reproduction of Texts

The text of No. 2 is reprinted by permission of Hanssler-Verlag, 7303 Neuhausen-Stuttgart, West Germany. The texts of Nos. 111 and 124 are reprinted by permission of B. Feldman & Co. Ltd, 138-140 Charing Cross Road, London, WC2H 0LD. For permission to reproduce these texts locally, application should be made to the addresses given above. For all other texts, applicants in the United States of America and Canada should apply to Hope Publishing Company, Carol Stream, Illinois 60188, USA. Applicants in the rest of the world should apply to Stainer & Bell Limited, 82 High Road, London N2 9PW, England.

Bibliography

Those publications named in the notes to the hymns are listed below:

100 Hymns for Today Hymns Ancient & Modern Limited, 16 Commerce Way, Colchester, Essex, CO2 8HH, England.

Break not the Circle Hope Publishing Company, Carol Stream, Illinois 60188, USA.

Canadian Hymnbook Offices of the Synod, Anglican Church of Canada, 600 Jarvis Street, Toronto, M4Y 2J6, Canada.

Cantate Domino Oxford University Press, Ely House, 37 Dover Street, London, W1, England.

Choir Book for Saints and Singers Agape, Hope Publishing Company, Carol Stream, Illinois 60188, USA.

Congregational Praise United Reformed Church, 86 Tavistock Place, London, WC1H 9RJ, England.

Ecumenical Praise Agape, Hope Publishing Company, Carol Stream, Illinois 60188, USA.

English Hymnal Oxford University Press, Ely House, 37 Dover Street, London, W1, England.

Hymns and Psalms Methodist Publishing House, Wellington Road, London, SW19, England.

Hymns and Songs Methodist Publishing House, Wellington Road, London, SW19, England.

Hymnal Supplement Hope Publishing Company, Carol Stream, Illinois 60188, USA.

Lieder zum Kirchentag Escherheimer Landstrasse 565, 6 Frankfurt am Main 50, Federal Republic of Germany.

New Catholic Hymnal Faber Music Limited, 3 Queen Square, London, WC1N 3AU, England.

New Church Praise Saint Andrew Press, 121 George Street, Edinburgh, EH2 4YN Scotland.

New Songs of Asian Cities Christian Conference of Asia, Urban Industrial Mission Department, 1-551-54 Totsuka, Shinjuku-ku, Tokyo-160, Japan.

Oxford Book of Carols Oxford University Press, Walton Street, Oxford, England.

Pilgrim Praise Stainer & Bell Limited, 82 High Road, London, N2 9PW, England.

Songs and Hymns from Sweden Stainer & Bell Limited, 82 High Road, London, N2 9PW, England.

Songs for the Seventies Stainer & Bell Limited, 82 High Road, London, N2 9PW, England.